PLATO

N. JAYAPALAN

ATLANTIC PUBLISHERS AND DISTRIBUTORS

Published by
ATLANTIC PUBLISHERS AND DISTRIBUTORS
B-2, Vishal Enclave, Opp. Rajouri Garden, New Delhi-27
Phones : 5413460, 5429987

Sales Office
4215/1, Ansari Road, Darya Ganj,
New Delhi-110 002
Phones : 3273880, 3285873, 3280451
Fax : 91-11-3285873
e-mail : gupta.atlantc@axcess.net.in

Typeset at
APD Computer Graphics, Delhi

Printed in India at
Mehra Offset Press, Delhi

PREFACE

It gives me a great pleasure to place this book in the hands of the readers. I am fully aware of the fact that there is a good number of excellent books on Plato and the History of Western political thought written by eminent English and American Scholars but they do not meet the requirements of the Indian students. So, in order to facilitate the task of the students of Indian universities and to enable the laymen to have an understanding and knowledge of many political ideas I have written this book.

In writing this book I do not claim any originality but at the same time my own political training has enabled me to give my own interpretation of events and facts on many issues. I have tried my best to maintain an impartial attitude in the exposition of various doctrines. My aim has been throughout to give students and laymen an easily intelligible exposition of various political ideas and institutions of Plato.

The subject has been dealt with in a very simple and lucid language. I take this opportunity of acknowledging my top indebtedness to various great and eminent scholars and teachers of Political Science from whose works I have borrowed freely and profusely.

I am thankful to the M/s Atlantic Publishers and Distributors, New Delhi for readily agreeing to publish this book and bringing it out expeditiously and efficiently.

Any suggestions, for the improvement of the book, are always welcomed and shall be gratefully acknowledged in the next edition.

N. JAYAPALAN

Contents

1

Introduction

Plato the philosopher, politician, mathematician, poet and reformer was born in 427 B. C. and died in 347 B.C. He was born in an aristocratic family of Athens, two years after the death of Pericles. He was related to Solon, the Law-Giver. The name of his father was Ariston. His mother was Perictione. His early name was Aristocles but he was later given the nickname of Plato.

As a free-born Athenian boy, Plato's early education consisted of a two-fold course of training in music and gymnastics. Ho excelled as a soldier and won many prizes in games.

Plato remained Socrates' pupil for eight years till the latter 's death. He was tremendously influenced by his master and evolved from a soldier to a philosopher. Will Durant has well said : "Philosophers are not apt to develop out of such adolescence. But Plato's subtle soul had found a new joy in the 'dialectic' game of Socrates; it was a delight to behold the master deflating dogmas and functioning presumptions with his sharp point of his question."

In 407 B.C. Plato joined the Socratic school to learn philosophy under the guidance of his old master Socrates. The turning point in his life came in the year 397 B.C., when he was twenty years old. In that year, his master was put on trial before the Athenian Courts on charges of disbelieving in the gods of the city of introducing new deities and of corrupting the youth. He refused to compromise and was condemned to death. He accepted the sentence with great calmness. Plato was profoundly shocked with the death of his master. So he decided not to take part in active politics, the career for which he was brought up. He spent his life in teaching and writing, in order to reform man and society. In other words he turned as teacher, writer, publisher and philosopher.

Plato founded his own Academy in Athens in 387 B.C. where it was his habit to meet his pupils. From then onwards his life was devoted to reflected literary publications and travel. Mathematics, Music, Jurisprudence and

Science were mainly taught in the Academy. He is said to have visited Africa, Egypt, Persia, Babylonia, the Hebrew people besides Italy and Sicily.

Plato was influenced by Megarian and Pythagorean doctrines, although he drew his chief inspiration from Socrates. His literary activity took the form of dialogues in which he represented conversations of Socrates with various interlocutors. "These were probably intended at first," writes Foster, "as memorials of Socrates; but more and more they became vehicles of Plato's own development of his master's thought, and it is now impossible to distinguish with certainty between what is Socratic and what is Platonic in the philosophy of the Platonic Socrates."

His Academy was both a school as well as an institute of scientific research, Students flocked to it from far and wide.

The Academy served two purposes: in the first place, "It served as an organisation of pure research." In the second place, "The Academy was also a school of political training, from which statesmen and legislators issued." Plato sought to impart knowledge which should be a way and an inspiration of life. It was through this academy that Plato aimed to restore the ancient glories of Greece through his disciples.

The Socratic doctrines that Virtue was knowledge and the Ideal was the real lie at the basis of Plato's philosophy — *i.e.* he identified virtue with knowledge. It was knowledge that moulded and disciplined the will and emotions and virtues like courage and temperance and justice flowed from knowledge. Another doctrine that Plato adopted from Socrates was the doctrine of the ideal being the real. His ideas concerning the state also underwent considerable change during the course of his life and are all tinged with his poetic and idealistic attitude of mind. He combined politics and ethics, devoting chief attention to the ends which the state should set before itself and viewing politics as the art of making man more just and virtuous.

Plato was a versatile genius. He dived deep into the ocean of knowledge and proved to be the father of many branches of science. He was the first great systematic philosopher. He was also a great mathematician and poet. He died at an advanced age of 80 at a wedding feast.

2

The Republic of Plato

The Republic of Plato is known as his masterpiece. It is also known as treatise of justice. It is a treatise on political science and jurisprudence.

Rousseau called The Republic a treatise on education.

In the words of Sabine, "Its range of subject matter is such that it may be said to deal with the whole of human life."

Plato's Works

There is a list of 36 dialogues of Plato. There is now almost a general agreement that every dialogue of any length and interest in this list is Platonic. These dialogues were written in different periods of his life and represent different phases in the evolution of his thought. His earliest dialogues, Socratic in touch and substance, include Euthyphro, Apology, Crito, Charmides, Lachos, Lysis, Euthymedus, Protagoras, Gorgias, Meno and possibly also Symposium and Phaedo. The dialogues, written when he was at the Academy and representing what is characteristic of Plato, include the Republic, Phaedus, Theactitus and Parmenides. Some of his last dialogues, written in the last years of his life, are Sophistes, Politicus, Timacus, Critias and Laws. The authenticity of the Republic is borne out by contemporary evidence and is not seriously questioned. A like authenticity can be established for the Laws, particularly due to Aristotle's testimony. The Politicus is slightly more doubtful but very probably was written in between the Republic and the Laws.

Schlerimacher holds that all the dialogues of Plato "are but parts of a general and constant plan which existed from the first in Plato's mind." Many recent students of Plato have been unable to accept this view.

Plato's works lack definite statements and precise conceptions about state as necessary for a coherent science of politics. According to Sir Frederick Pollock, "Platonic Republic, I think, must be considered as a brilliant exercise of philosophical imagination, not as a contribution to political science.....Plato never got to the point of having a theory of the state at all."

The Republic

The Republic of Plato, translated from the Greek word Politeia, does not mean republic in the ordinary sense of the work but means a political constitution in general. It is the longest of his works and is certainly the greatest of them. It was written in the maturity of Plato's life, *i.e.,* at the age of 40. The Republic is the centre round which other dialogues of Plato may be grouped. In no other dialogues Plato shows the same largeness of view, the same perfection of style, the same knowledge of the world. The more you read of it, the more you are struck by the astonishing genius of Plato, his great speculative powers, his wit and the universality of his interests. According to Bhandari, "It is the parent of idealism in philosophy; in politics and in education."

The Republic is, as Nettleship puts it, a dramatized philosophy of human life. "The whole Republic is really an attempt to interpret human nature psychologically : the postulate upon which its method rests is that all the instructions of society, class organisation, law, religion, art and so on, are ultimately products of the human soul, an inner principle of life which works itself out in these outward shapes."

In the Republic, Plato draws a picture of what the social organisations and institutions must be if an individual is to realise fully his highest capacities. It is the foundation study of the moral and civic life of man. To Stallbaum, the Republic aimed at "the representation of human life in a state perfected by justice, and governed according to the idea of good." The Republic no doubt, projects an ideal society and is a Utopia but it also embodies a penetrating criticism of actual conditions of society in the days of Plato. For this bold criticism, The Republic has been called an indictment of Greek Civilisation. It is definitely written with full consciousness of the failure of Athens and of the deteriorators of the Greek City-state which was happening in Plato's life time. The book is indeed a treatise on social and political reforms. It is also the representation of the noblest and the best in life. According to Crossman, "It contains Plato's plan for the building of a perfect state in which every citizen is really happy." According to Sabine, "Few books that claim to be treatises on politics are clearly reasoned or so well co-ordinated as The Republic. None, perhaps, contains a line of thought so bold, so original, or so provocative. It is this quality which has made it a book for all time, from which later ages have drawn the most varied inspiration." To the end the polity depicted in the Republic remains Plato's ideal and the schemes propounded in the Politicus and the Laws represent his second best.

Principal Characters

The principal characters in the Republic are Cephalus, Polemarchus, Thracymachus, Glaucon, Adeimantus and Socrates. The first three drop out by the end of the first Book and the main discussion is carried on by the last three.

The Republic discusses problems from three points of view, *i.e.,* "that the unphilosophical decent representative of current convention, sustained by Cephalus and his son Polemarchus; that of the 'new morality', represented by Thracymachus; and that of sober philosophical thinking represented by Socrates."

The portrayal of Socrates in this Republic is not wholly consistent. For instance, his antagonism to the Sophists softens in the latter books of the dialogue.

From the point of view of Socrates and of Plato there is no distinction between Ethics and Politics. The ethical laws are the same for individuals and communities. These laws are primarily norms of personal morality giving a man the rule of right by which to regulate his life. They give politics an ethical basis. They are more easily discoverable in Politics than in Ethics because they are 'Writ large' in the former.

The Republic starts with the fundamental question : What is justice? This is because it was Plato's aim to construct a "moral order for the realisation of the virtue of justice which embraces all other virtues." The Republic is thus a treatise on human nature and human soul and deals with the important question of Law to live best.

According to Plato the states take their character from the characters of the men in them. His Republic is a treatise on a complete philosophy of man. It is concerned with man in social action and is therefore, ethico-political in nature and substance.

To Plato, politics was not so much the art of administering laws, and maintaining peace and order but, primarily, the art of making men better. During the time of Plato life in Athens was more public than private. A good man was a good citizen and must live in a good state. This brought together psychology and social sciences.

No doubt problems of a good man and a good state were two facets of the same coin. A man is an integral part of the society. He cannot be good to himself without his goodness affecting the society. Ethics and Politics, therefore, are, inseparable according to Plato.

Viewpoints

Besides being a treatise on Ethics and Politics, it is one on metaphysics because it exhibits the unity of all things in the idea of the good. It deals with life after death and preparations for it. It represents a fine discourse on moral philosophy, because it investigates the virtues of the human soul and shows their union and perfection in justice.

Explaining as it does the process of historical change it is a treatise on the philosophy of history.

The Republic of Plato is no less a book on sociology and economics. His system of communism has its sociological and eugenic import.

Plato regulated the system of property and marriage for the improvement of society. To secure a better type of human breed, he resorts to state-controlled making and is even prepared to 'expose' undesirable children.

In the Republic there is a good deal of political economy. It gives us an economic theory of the origin of the state. Every individual has multifarious wants but limited capacities. It is not possible for them to meet all these wants by his own labour. This gives origin to a desire for economic cooperation between individuals on the basis of division of labour and specialisation of functions.

The Republic of Plato treads on religion too. Plato introduces the subject of the immortality of the soul in the second part of Book X. Plato asserts that the true nature and capacities of the soul cannot be soon in its earthly state.

Plato was aiming all an ideal state based on his conception of justice, the practical realisation of which depended on two things, *i.e.,* (1) a system of common education by the State and (2) communism.

The Republic is held to be Plato's masterpiece, the crowning achievement of his art and philosophy. In it, Plato explains his attitude towards the following fundamental problems :

(1) What is Good? What are the principles of right action and virtue?

What is justice? Taking justice to be the supreme virtue, he tried to visualise an ideal polity in which justice should reign supreme.

(2) Since, as Plato held, virtue was teachable, what educational system could best promote virtue?

(3) Who is a good man? How is a good man made?

(4) What is the best type of political organisation? *i.e.,* What is the good state? How is the good state made?

Here, moral philosophy moves into political science.

Criticism

The Republic contains a good deal of criticism on contemporary institutions, practices and opinions.

(1) According to Dunning "Plato's Republic is a mere romance."

(2) Barker says, "It is easy to interpret the Republic as a Utopia, a city in the clouds, a sunset fabric seen for an hour in the evening and then

fading into the night.....But the Republic is not a city of nowhere. It is based on actual conditions, it is meant to mould or at any rate to influence actual life."

(3) Some people think that it is an ironical work, "a Utopia to end all Utopias".

(4) It is written in a spirit of critical reform of social and political order.

(5) The Republic is a polemic against the current sophist teachers and contemporary politics. It attacks sophistic anarchism as well as democratic egalitarianism. The sophists preached the 'justice' of self-satisfaction. In opposition to this the Republic teaches the conception of justice as a quality of the soul which enables a citizen to sacrifice himself for the city-state.

Subject Matter of the Republic

There are five divisions. They are :

(1) *Book I and part of the Book II.* There are views about human life and of the nature of justice and the meaning of morality.

(2) *Books II, III and IV.* This division deals with the construction of the first state and the first system of education. Plato describes in outline, what could be the best form of human society, 'Justice' is to be traced to the institution of this society.

(3) *Books V, VI and VII.* In this division, philosophy rather than justice is the subject of enquiry. The second state is constructed on the principles of communism and is to be ruled by philosophers.

(4) *Books VIII and IX.* The perversions of the state and of the individuals are reviewed in this division.

(5) *Book X.* It contains two sections. In the first section, the relation of philosophy to art, especially to poetry is discussed in detail. In the second, Plato deals with the capabilities and destinies of the human soul.

The central part of the Republic is represented by Book V to the end of Book VII. The part is full of eloquence and imagination and is full of value and meaning for the metaphysician, the religious teacher, and the social, political and religious reformer in all ages and climes.

Later on the above views of Plato exercised a tremendous influence in the field of political thought in the world.

3

Plato's Ideal State

Plato's Theory of Ideas

Plato's Doctrine of Ideas is considered as the keystone of his political thought. The entire Greek political thought is nothing but a search for the ultimate reality. If to Thales water was the ultimate reality, it was the Infinite or Boundless for Anaximender and for Anaximenes air was the ultimate reality of the whole universe. To Pythagoras the abstract principle — the number was the ultimate reality. To Heraclitus it was change. Still to some others it was permanence or stability that was the real nature of all things. In the language of Paranindas being alone remains unmoved, which is the name for all. There was the absolute world of the one, unchanging, unified and eternal on one hand and on the other the shifting world of appearance, ceaselessly changing, eternally unreal, the real of non-being. Against this background of peculation Plato developed his Theory of Ideas.

The permanent character of a thing is what Plato calls the "Idea". This Idea of a thing is eternal and final, having no independent and absolute reality.

There are two worlds, *i.e.,* the world of Being and the world of Becoming. The first is static because it is a world of perfection; and the second is dynamic and imperfect.

The world of Being is the ideal world and such it is the real world. It is a world of universal concepts which are valid and true for all times and places. They are unchangeable, imperishable and eternal. They are Real.

The world of Becoming is imperfect and unreal. It is in a constant state of change and flux. The world of Being is realised through Reason and that of Becoming through sense perceptions. The world of Being is Ideal, that of Becoming is Actual.

It is the Ideal alone which is real and not the Actual. The Actual is not real because it is in a constant state of flux. It has no stability on consistency and, therefore, reality. No actual state can be real because it is constantly undergoing social, economic and political changes. It is only an ideal state, a perfect state based on universal and eternal principles which can be real. The Ideal lies behind the Actual and is the goal to which the Actual tries to evolve. Thus, there is a telelogical connection between the Ideal and the Actual.

The Actual world is not only constantly changing but its knowledge is based on sense-perceptions which are imperfect, subjective, unreliable, inconsistent and, therefore, unreal. Reality can only be with the Ideal which is realised through Reason which is objective.

Plato portrays the picture of an Ideal state very beautifully in his masterpiece "The Republic". The object of his Ideal state is the good life and in his effort to portray the Good, Plato pursues his thought to their almost limits, "even in the end beyond time and space to the vision of reality which may not be in this world." Plato tries to achieve his idea of the Good by the establishment of a state which is free from the evil of all other states because it does not degenerate, or because it does not change. The state which is free from the evil of change and corruption is the best; it is the perfect state. It is the state of the Golden Age.

Plato's Republic is a Utopia in the sense that in it Plato depicted a state which was, primarily an embodiment of the "Idea of the Good". Plato wanted the future statesman to know from him what 'Good' was and how to construct a 'Good State'. His Ideal state was meant to be the state as such, a type or model for all places and all times.

Plato's belief is perfect and unchanging things is usually called his theory or doctrine of forms of Ideas. It constitutes the central doctrine of his philosophy. It is on this theory of the Idea, that the rest of the theories of the Ideal state are based. According to Edman, "The Platonic idea is the original and the original of the thing, the reason of its existence — the stable, sustaining principle in virtue of which it exists. It is the virtue of the thing, its ideal, its perfection."

Thus, Plato's discovery of ideas as the ultimate reality has led to the development of the concept of two worlds — the world of objects and the world of Ideas. The first world is unreal and the world of ideas is the real world. The first world is only the world of shadow. Of the ideas, Plato calls the idea of Good and the final and independent reality existing 'itself by itself'. It is the source of all goodness. It is by virtue of participation in it that men are good. It is only in following after good that men will find respite from their many afflictions.

Plato's Ideal State

Plato constructs his Ideal State in three successive 'waves'. In the first wave he shows that men and women should have the same education and should partake in the same public functions. In the second wave he advocates the abolition of the family on the basis of communism of wives and property among the two upper classes. The third wave is concerned with the idea that the salvation of society depended on government by Philosopher kings.

Plato's Ideal State is hierarchical in its composition and functioning.

Features

(1) *Rule of Philosophy* : According to Plato, "If political power and scientific knowledge (philosophy) are not united in one person, then there is no end of evil for the States and also for mankind in general". According to him his Ideal State will be guided by eternal ideas and the life is to be governed by the absolute ideas. This life of Becoming is to be made life of Being. Only philosophers can understand these ideas. Hence, the ruler will be able to rule the State according to these ideas. Reason will dominate as the chief quality of the Philosopher-guardians.

So at the head of Plato's Ideal State there is a Philosopher-ruler who would be the embodiment of reason and, therefore, virtue in action, whose wise and beneficent rule is untrammelled by the restraints of law. This implies that the philosopher-ruler knows the art of statesmanship and state-craft.

A Philosopher King is a true statesman and his monarchy is the best form of Government. He has the decisive power in Government and it is his knowledge alone which entitles him to the position. His knowledge is at once his right and duty to rule. The Philosopher-rulers are, according to Plato, the men of gold, whom nature has given birth to rule.

(2) *State-regulated Education* : Plato suggests a well regulated scheme of education under state control in order to ensure a constant supply of philosophers-guardians. State was, to him, to be mainly an educational institution. All the rulers must pass through this established and State controlled system of training and education. They are trained to acquire higher knowledge. The curriculum is to be consisted of subjects such as Mathematics. Astronomy, Logic and Dialectics. In the elementary education he includes training in gymnastics and music for the perfection of body and mind. This system is to train individuals from their boyhood upto the age of 35 and thus they become real and true philosophers of the design which Plato desires. Moreover, it would be possible to shift the capable from the incapable. Plato takes care to divide the guardian class into perfect guardians "who preserve as against foreign enemies and maintain peace among our citizens at home" and auxiliaries or administrators who are mere supporters of the perfect guardians.

(3) *Communism of Wives and Property* : Plato is of the opinion that the philosopher, freed from the cares of his family and private property will devote more attention to the affairs of the state and to the cultivation and

acquisition of sound knowledge. The communism of wives and property among the upper classes *i.e.*, guardian classes was meant to keep them out of the economic and worldly temptations and ambitions so that they could concentrate on their duty to the State.

(4) *Vocational Specialisation* : Plato divides the whole community into three classes or professions. Firstly, there is the class of philosopher guardians, *i.e.,* perfect rulers representing Reason. They are fit for the highest duties of statesmanship. Secondly, there were ordinary guardians, *i.e.,* auxiliaries and administrators representing the element of spirit. Lastly, there are non-guardians, *i.e.,* common people. They are otherwise called producing class, cut up into a number of sections such as artisans and farmers, each with its own special work. The specialisation of functions is based on two factors — natural aptitude and training. The first is innate and the second is matter of experience and education.

(5) *Justice* : Justice is a cornerstone of Plato's Ideal State. To him, a State was Ideal if justice reigns supreme in it. The philosopher-ruler knows what is justice. He should foster justice in an appropriate manner. According to him unity and harmony will prevail in the State because of justice and it is inseparable from his Ideal State. It grows with the specialisation of functions. The justice of the State is the citizen's sense of duty.

(6) *Equality of Men and Women* : Plato gives same status to men and women in his Ideal State. To him, the day of emancipation of women will be the day of unity of the State, liberty to the individual and justice to both. He gives his whole-hearted support for this. He plans to give the same education to both sexes.

(7) *Censorship of Art and Literature* : The Ideal State of Plato is absolute and totalitarian. Plato is no apostle of freedom of thought and association. Even the art and literature which goes against the interest of the State must be destroyed. He advocates a strict censorship of art and literature.

To him, the State is Ideal and is ruled by supreme wisdom.

Criticism

The following criticisms have been levelled against the Ideal State of Plato :

(1) In his organistic conception and construction of the Ideal State, Plato finds too much analogy between the individual and the State which leads to confusion.

(2) His classification of human nature into three elements, *viz.*, Reason, Spirit and Appetite and his subsequent division of society into three classes — guardians, auxiliaries and the producing class — is rather illogical and false.

(3) Plato fails to distinguish Ethics from Politics. He builds a dream city in which the city and citizen become one.

(4) In his state, which is collectivist, there is very little scope for full freedom and all around development of the various faculties of man.

(5) His stress on functional specialisation and his idea of justice are likely to dwarf the personality of an individual. It condemns an individual to a single function in life. There is need for development of man as a whole and not as a part.

(6) Hegel criticises Plato's Ideal State on the score that it allows no subjective freedom.

(7) The producing classes are ignored altogether as if they are soulless. He neither advocates nor makes any provision for their emancipation.

(8) Plato overestimates intellect and under-estimates character as if the most intellectual were the most virtuous.

(9) He equates, the State with the ruling class. His men of brass and iron are doomed to remain brass and iron because his educational scheme is meant only for the guardian class.

(10) Plato fails to denounce slavery, which was so rampant in his days.

(11) Plato's communism of wives and property is most intolerable. It violates human nature and instincts. His system of temporary marriages is most unworkable.

(12) The rule of philosophy and of philosopher kings is unrealisable. To make the philosopher king above law is to make him most absolute and authoritarian. It is nothing but espousing the cause of the worst type of dictatorship.

(13) Plato's conception of Rule of Philosophy goes against the spirit of democracy, equality and liberty. It assigns sovereign power permanently to persons, one or few, instead of to law. Power first concentrates and then it corrupts. Consequently it is bound to degenerate into enlightened tyranny.

(14) In his portrait of the Ideal State, Plato has ignored the most important needs of the community, such as rules and regulations for the appointment of officials, rules regarding instituting of courts, etc.

(15) Plato's principle that the State is everything and that it can and should control absolutely the entire lives of citizens is absurd.

(16) Plato's polity is 'intolerant, absolute and impracticable'. But no one knows what the absolute ideas are.

(17) Aristotle criticised the Ideal State of Plato on various grounds. Plato's communism of property was against human nature. Plato aimed at perfect unity in the state but complete unity was ruinous to the state for the very nature of the state was plurality. Real unity lay in proper organisation of relations between dissimilar individuals. Aristotle also critizised Plato for his neglect of the lower classes. This neglect might divide the society and the state into two hostile camps.

No wonder his Ideal State has profoundly influenced human thought and practice in spite of many criticisms. It has provoked a number of subsequent Utopias. Modern political practice has tried at least partly, to realise the pattern provided by Plato's Ideal State. Communism, functional specialisation and rule of intellect are some of the most important features of Plato's Ideal State.

Above all the most important contribution of Plato in this State is that he brought moralisation of ethics with the activities of the State. As Catlin says, "He (Plato) ethicised politics." Sabine remarks that he tried to find a type of state in which all the sociological forces worked in harmony.

4

Plato's Conception of Justice

The primary issue of the Republic is the discovery of the nature and habitation of justice. The Republic, therefore, is called a treatise on justice.

Dr. Barker has rightly said: "Justice is the hinge of his (Plato's) thought and the text of his discourse."

During his days incompetence and factionalism, unrighteousness and injustice and ignorance reigned supreme. So, Plato was keen to find out a solution to all these evils and injustice he found the remedy of curing these evils.

Plato first reviews and discards the various old theories of justice and then constructs his own.

To Plato and his contemporary Greeks, the word justice conveyed a meaning different from the one it carries nowadays. The Greek word for justice is *dikaisune* which has wider implication than the English word 'justice' and comes very near the English word 'morality'. It represents a disposition to do the right thing. To us, justice is mainly associated with judicial and administrative acts.

The Traditional Theory of Justice

This theory was propounded by Cephalus and Polemarchus. According to this theory justice meant being true in world and action and paying one's debts to gods and men. Thus, justice meant giving due, that is to say, doing good to friends and harm to enemies.

This view is criticised by Plato on the ground that there may be many cases in which to adhere to the latter of this formula may involve the violation of the spirit of right, and this formula does not admit of being taken as a sound universal principle of life.

Socrates refutes this theory by saying that firstly it is not justice that enables one to be good to one's friends and bad to foes, but knowledge of things, and secondly, that appearances are often deceptive, your supposed friends or foes may not be really so and lastly that on no account it can be maintained that injuring a person, even your enemies, is against morality and cannot be called justice. Thus, the conventional views of justice, held by Cephalus and Polemarchus, regulates relations between individuals on individualistic principles and ignored the society. True justice, to Plato, connotes the spirit of service which involves an idea of a social to which this service could be rendered.

Sophists Theory of Justice

Thrasymachus is a typical representative of radical sophists. He represents the new and critical views about the nature of morality and justice. He, in sophistical spirit accuses Socrates as juggler of words and demands accuracy in the argument. He overstates his case and is lost in consequent confusion. To him, justice is the interest of thc stronger. He explains it by saying that army government takes law and enforces them with its coercive power for the benefit of the sovereign. These laws represent justice which is meted out to the subjects who if they break these laws are accused as unjust and punished. In a state the Government is the strongest, it will try to get and it will get, whatever it wants for itself. The standard of action in a State is, therefore, the will of the ruler, who wills his own good. As such, justice is synonymous will what is expedient for the rulers.

The implications of this definition of justice needs examination. In the first place, it identifies might with right. Justice of the State looks after its own interest, *i.e.,* the interest of the all powerful ruler. But what is just for one man, *i.e.,* the ruler, must be just for others too. Therefore, every man must look after his own interest. Justice, thus, consists in obeying the laws of the State when one must and following one's own interest where one can. Secondly from the point of view of the ordinary man, justice is another man's good; it is deemed unjust to pursue one's own good if that involves a breach of the laws. But every one by a law of nature seeks his own good, according to Thracymachus, injustice is better than justice and so all sensible persons should follow the former as it brings wisdom, strength and happiness. Socrates (Plato) counters this by pointing out that it is justice that brings wisdom and happiness born of one's knowledge of one's limitations. Justice is not the interest of the stronger. The Governors are just shepherds to protect their sheep and exit for the good of the governed and, therefore, justice is the interest of the weaker, *i.e.,* the governed and not of the stronger, *i.e.,* the sovereign. Here, are germs of one of the cardinal tenets of modern politics, *i.e.,* 'Power is a trust'. Justice produces social harmony by developing socially expedient behaviour.

Glaucon's Theory

Glaucon carries on the argument of Thracymachus. This theory regards justicc as "the interest of the weaker. It is a child of fear. It is a mean or compromise among the best of all, which is to do injustice and not be punished and the worst of all, which is to suffer justice without the power of retaliation." The weaker, fearing more injustice than they can inflict, instituted law and government through a sort of social contract. It is through this artificial rule of justice and law that the natural selfishness of man is chained — a dictate of the weaker many, for the interest of the weaker many, as against the natural and superior power of the stronger few.

This theory is also rejected by Plato. According to Plato justice is not conventional or external. It is the right condition of human soul and is something internal. It is found both in the state and the individual. It is natural and not artificial. It is not born of fear of the weak but of the longing of the human soul to do a duty according to its nature.

Plato's Conception of Justice

Having rejected the various theories of justice, Plato propounds his own theory of justice which is true and final through the person of Socrates. He gives extraordinary importance to justice, as is obvious from the sub-title of his best dialogue, The Republic, because he saw injustice, the only remedy against the political and social ills of his beloved city-state Athens. Justice, according to Plato resides in the ideally constituted community and is identifiable with complete virtue which consists of four virtues, *i.e.*, wisdom (Philosophers), courage (which includes strength of will), obedience and discipline (soldiers), temperance or self-control and justice. To Plato "Justice is the virtue which remains in the state when the other virtues of temperance and courage and wisdom are abstracted and is the ultimate cause and condition of the existence of all of them." The conception of justice is inseparable from that of the Ideal State. The two blend in one and cannot be isolated. Justice is the order, *i.e.,* the true condition of the state, and the Ideal State is the visible embodiment of justice. The one is the soul, the other the body-fair mind in a fair body.

A good and just life is one lived in society and justice demands an organic unity in the state arising out of a harmonious balancing of functions of the three classes of society : the appetitive, the spirited and the rational and justice in Plato's language means "the will to concentrate on one's own sphere of duty and not to meddle with the sphere of others and its habitation, therefore, is the heart of every citizen who does his duty in his appointed place". Thus, justice depends and grows with the specialisation of functions. "The justice of the state is the citizens' sense of duty." To Plato, justice is an indispensable quality of moral life in the community. Platonic justice does not embody a conception of individual rights; it conceives of individual duties. Plato's polity is a moral organism and his theory of justice is a theory of the ethical code by which it lives.

Justice of the Individual

Justice of the individual means that each of the three elements — appetite, spirit and reason — keep within their proper limits. Justice of the individual is both a public and a private virtue because it maintains the highest good of both the society and the individual.

To Plato, justice in the individual is identifiable with virtue or excellence. It is virtue as man, *i.e.,* human virtue and not mere functional virtue that makes him "good". Justice or virtue which makes a man *good* is analysed by Plato into its constituent elements of wisdom, courage, temperance and justice. Justice is architectonic in relation to other excellences and is necessary for their perfection. It permeates them, harmonises them and keep them within proper bounds, just as an architect keeps craftsmen like masons and carpenters within proper limits. It generates the spirit of self-restraint and self-regulation in the individual and makes him a useful member of society. Justice, is thus, not a purely 'personal' virtue but has a social side too. It is a bond of societies and states. It holds men together in healthy social relationship by making them good and making them social.

Legal Justice

Plato also makes a distinction between legal or particular and perfect or universal justice. The perfect justice can only be in the Ideal State which is based on right education, principle of communism, functional specialisation and perfect wisdom of a philosopher-king. In a State which is not Ideal and which is based on law, there obtains legal or particular justice. Plato's idea of distributive justice is that men should get offices according to their devotion to the State. Ability included moral and intellectual ability.

Criticism

Platonic conception of justice has been criticised in many ways :

(1) It is based on self-control and self abnegation of the individual in the interests of the society.

(2) Plato's concept of justice does not provide for class of individual wills and conflict between one interest and another. It envisages a dual uniformity and harmony of social life.

(3) It is a system of duties and not of right of the individuals and yet the two must always be correlated in a healthy society.

(4) The theory is based on the conception of functional specialisation, but it ignores its evils. It does not sufficiently realise and properly provide for the 'whole' of human personality. To condemn a man to one special function is to assume that he is all appetite on all reason, whereas an average man has all the three elements in him. The ideal of 'one man one work'

militates against the full development of human personality and deprives the community of a full and rich variety of life. Platonic justice is static and passive. It is too subjective, hence, it is no justice at all. It does not issue forth in a concrete judicial organisation.

(5) Through his theory of justice the reconciliation, Plato attempts to effect between self-interest and public duty is not very satisfactory. It is a system of duties only. Rights are ignored altogether.

(6) Platonic justice fails to promote the happiness of all. According to Aristotle, "Plato in The Republic deprives the guardians of happiness, and says that the legislator ought to make the whole state happy. But the whole cannot be happy unless most, or all, or some of its parts, enjoy happiness."

(7) Plato's justice gives a monopoly of political power to one class *i.e.,* philosophers only. Such a monopoly of political power in the hands of one class, however well-trained morally and spiritually, is bound to demoralise that class, sooner or later, and corrupt the state. Zeller criticises it as aristocratic contempt. But Salime remarks that "his treatment is only a logical conclusion of his assumption". It exposes the philosopher-rulers to the temptation of identifying public interests with their own class interests.

(8) The Platonic justice with communism of wives and property ignores the essentials of human psychology and denies satisfaction to the fundamental carvings of the human soul. The whole concept is impracticable and unrealisable.

(9) It is static. It assigns a man a particular position in life and condemns him to that position throughout his life. According to Will Durant, Plato is too anxious to have a moving picture of this world became a fixed and still tableau. He loves order exclusively like any timid philosopher as he has been frightened by the democratic turbulence of Athens into an extreme neglect of individual value.

(10) It is said that Plato has sacrificed the individual for the sake of efficiency. But Wayper does not agree with this because according to him, "For Plato the state is efficient because it is just, it is not just because it is efficient."

(11) Plato does not say anything about freedom. As a matter of fact Plato's philosophy of justice "is the most savage and the most profound attack upon liberal ideas which history can show. It denies every axiom of progressive thought and challenges all

its fondest ideals. Equality, freedom, self-government, all are condemned as illusions which can be held by idealists whose sympathies are stronger than their sense," writes Crossman.

(12) It is too subjective and does not issue in an objective law for the guidance of the people.

The Value of His Theory

In spite of above criticism, Plato's theory of justice is of immense value. It is a kind of thesis against individualism. "The conception postulates a view of the individual as not an isolated self, but part of an order, intended not to pursue the pleasure of isolated self, but to fill an appointed place in that order."

Plato's justice is universal in character and is another name for the whole duty of men.

According to Dunning, the Platonic conception of justice "on the political side proper brings out in highest relief, first, the necessity of an organic unity in social life; second, the importance of systematic education, as contrasted with the haphazard legislation in regulating the common interest; and third, the national basis of aristocracy in government."

Plato's theory bestows upon the state a personality and independent existence of its own. There is no doubt that the theory is a revolt against political selfishness and ignorance.

Justice in Plato is a part of human virtue and also a bond of state at the same time. It is that bond which joins man together in society. It makes man both good and social. "This identification is the first and the fundamental principle of Plato's political philosophy" according to Foster. This conception also gave birth to the organic theory of the state. In a way it also resolves the problem of individual liberty and the Leviathan state. It brings the final identification between the individual and the society to which he is born.

The conception is of importance also due to the fact that it brings into prominence two important principles of division of labour and specialisation of function for efficiency and harmony in the state.

Moreover, the significance of Plato's theory lies in the fact that it is the forerunner of the psychological explanation of the state. States do not come out of a rock, they grow from the characters of men.

5

Plato on the Rule of Philosophy

Plato deals with the Rule of Philosophy in Books V and VI of the Republic. "If political power and scientific knowledge (Philosophy) are not united in one person, then there is no end of evil for the states and also for mankind in general." In this statement Plato sums up his views regarding the government of the Ideal State which must rest with philosophers. Plato was thoroughly disgusted with the evils of Athenian democracy and he found solvation only in the rule of the philosopher-kings. In books VIII and IX of the Republic Plato reviews a number of states if only to condemn them.

In Plato's portrayal of the Ideal State, the system of government was a natural corollary of the system of education. The government flowed from education, not education from the government. The government must be directed and controlled by knowledge and because the only true knowledge was philosophy, the government must be controlled by philosophers.

According to Plato only by the rule of the Philosopher-kings can the stake a government in which the rulers rule in wisdom and in unselfishness for their eyes have seen the truth and they think of their exalted offices not as opportunities for self-aggrandisement but as a sacred burden to be borne for the good of the ruled.

His Conception of a Philosopher

Plato conceives of a philosopher as "the spectator of all time and all existence". "He has the noblest gifts of nature and makes the highest use of them." He is a lover of truth and has always a passion for reality. He hates falsehood and possesses self-control. He is free from all sorts of meanness or spitefulness or little-mindedness. He is just and gentle and shows due proportion in all things. He does not fear death or think much of human life. He has a vision of the unity of knowledge. The Platonic Philosopher must know the "Idea" or essence of justice, and of Beauty and Temperance in order that he may fashion with their likeness the characters of those whom he rules, ultimately he must know the "Idea" of which all other Ideas are but phases and from which above comes the "Idea of the

Good". He must know the purpose of all-being and all-doing and the end of all human existence and human action.

The Platonic philosopher, however, is not the devoted seeker for wisdom but its proud possessor; he is a learned man and a sage. By the rule of philosophy, Plato means the rule of learnedness or the rule of the intellect. It is in this rule of intellect that the Socratic doctrine of 'knowledge is virtue' is fully realised in its institutional form.

According to Popper, "Plato gives the term philosopher a new meaning of a lover and a seer of the divine world of forms or Ideas". It is this philosopher who becomes the virtuous founder of a virtuous city.

The Philosopher King

By creating the philosopher-king Plato made an attempt to create a friend, a philosopher and a guide at the same time who could, by leading a life of ascetic simplicity and virtue, inspire confidence among his subjects.

Plato's philosopher-king is similar to the ancient Indian Rajarishi who is the embodiment of all knowledge, all virtue, all beauty and all divinity.

Appetite, to Plato, was a social bond, bringing men together for the satisfaction of their wants; spirit gave safety and integrity but these two were not enough without a regulative force. Uncontrolled appetite would lead to unbridled political and economic individualism and unbridled spirit would produce unmitigated brutes. Reason was necessary regulative force and the philosopher rulers embodied reason.

Limitations on the Philosopher-King

Although the philosopher-king was to be absolute ruler untrammalled by written Laws, but he was not free of all restraints. He must respect the fundamentals of the states, which he must not radically change in a hurry and at his own sweet will. These fundamentals relate to :

(i) regulation of wealth and property in the State;

(ii) the size of the State;

(iii) the rule of justice and

(iv) system of education.

Thus, the philosopher-king of Plato was the servant of a fundamental social order.

Plato's philosopher-king would be above laws and above selfishness; and would render to every man his due, not the due of non-existent 'average man' which the law provides for. He will rule the state in accordance with his own free judgement and will be responsible to his own conscience alone. A philosopher-king should be more burdened with laws than a medical practitioner with medical rules. Plato was, therefore, in favour of the monarchy of a philosopher-king ruler.

Aristocracy of Intellect

Plato's system of education was calculated to produce a class of intellectuals who, known as Guardians, would rule the state. This naturally meant the creation of an aristocracy of intellect. His best preference was for a philosopher-king. According to Plato there were other men who fairly well qualified the philosopher-king in insight, education and excellence of character, the philosopher king should share his rule with them by some suitable arrangement. In short he was in favour of government by the expertly bred and educated and the modern services may be said to be looking upto this Ideal.

Criticism

Plato's philosophy has been subject to the following severe criticisms :

(1) By propounding this theory, Plato ignored altogether the Greek conception of the state as being an association of equals, having only the sovereignty of law.

(2) His 'new monarchy' was likely to degenerate into an 'enlightened' and 'beneficial tyranny'.

(3) The moral value of freedom and civic virtues of self-government are altogether ignored by Plato.

(4) Plato's theory ruled out direct as well as representative democracy.

(5) Plato does not propose for his philosopher-statesman any study of finance or law or military tactics but only of abstract mathematics and dialectics, we do not know how they are useful to run the government. We do not come across such philosopher-rulers in history.

(6) A philosopher-ruler may be too much given to contemplation to take decisive action when such action is urgently needed, as for instance in the case of an external attack or an internal political crisis. He may be so ignorant of realities of political life and of world in general as to fall an easy prey to the art and seduction of clever and unscrupulous people. Such philosopher-ruler is apt to fail even in the routine political life in the state.

(7) Excessive philosophic contemplation leads to eccentricity and the rule of an eccentric man is bound to be misunderstood, and, therefore, unpopular. It may be unjust and unbalanced.

(8) Plato's philosopher-kings are like modern dictators. Their unlimited powers will ruin the Ideal State. So Popper in his "Open Society and Enemies" states that his philosophy led to a closed world. It is due to the absolute powers of the philosopher-kings.

(9) Plato, on the whole remains an Utopian and his attempt at the creative of philosopher rulers remains a very difficult task to be achieved.

(10) We do not find anywhere in The Republic general principles of government. According to Jowett, "The philosopher-ruler is apt to be looking into the distant future or back into the remote past and unable to see actions and events of the present."

6

Plato's Theory of Communism

In his attempt to build an Ideal State in which justice should reign supreme Plato propounds a theory of a new social order, under which the governing class surrenders, in the interest of the state, both family life and private property and lives under a system of communism. His communism is not the central thesis of his philosophy. In the words of Barker, "It is only an outwork or bastion." His central theory is about justice and education. In order to realise them, his communism is only a necessity. It is only a material and economic corollary of the spiritual reformation, mainly the realisation of justice in the state. Hence, his communism is consequential, though by no means unimportant. It is meant to destroy the wrong notion of self as an isolated unit and replace it by the idea of a self as a useful and integral part of social whole.

Previous History of Communism

Plato's communistic doctrines were not entirely remote to his own land and generation. The idea of communism was known even before him.

There was the example of Sparta where wives were lent for state purpose, boys taken from their parents, at the age of seven, to be brought up by the state and where the ruling class had a common mess and lived to a certain extent, a common life.

In Crete there were public lands tilled by public serfs.

In Pythagorean dictum that "friends' goods were common goods" lent a theoretical support to communism.

In Athens, during the 5th century B.C. the Communistic theories definitely appeared to idealise the primitive nature people who held things common. The abolition of private property followed the general cynic doctrine of 'back to nature', Radical speculation, in contemporary Greece, attacked right of property in slaves and passed on to an attack on right of property in general.

Herodotus records how the Agathyseans have then women in common.

Basis of Plato's Communism

Plato advocated his communism on three grounds. It was the necessary result of his conception of justice in which everyone was supposed to perform his allotted function only. To Plato, the Community was all important and not the individual. Therefore, he wanted a citizen, confined to his allotted task, must merge himself in the state and tender specialised service to the state. Plato's ideal state consisted of three classes *i.e.*, (1) real rulers or guardians, (2) the auxiliaries or administrators and (3) all other social or professional groups not under the first two classes.

The upper two classes, *i.e.* guardians and auxiliaries including soldiers, must live under a regime of communism if they were to perform their duties well and unselfishly. These two classes represented the elements of reason and spirit. They must confine themselves to these elements and must renounce the element of appetite. They must, therefore, abnegate the economic side of life which was purely appetitive and relegate it to the farmers and artisans *etc.* Unless the appetite side is absolutely renounced, it may get the better of reason and may lead to personal ambition, selfish acquisition, neglect of duty, etc. Reason without communism, may remain dormant or inactive or may be impaired by appetite. The appetite may turn the watch-dog into a wolf.

The two upper classes must be made free from the worries and snares of economic and domestic life. Plato holds "Both the community of property and the community of families, as I am saying, tend to make them more truly guardians; they will not tear the city in pieces by differing about 'mine' and 'not mine', each man dragging any acquisitions which he has made into a separate house of his own, where he has a separate wife and children and private pleasures and pains; but all will be affected as far as may be by the same pleasures and pains because they are all of one opinion about what is demand near to them, and therefore, they all tend towards a common end. The guardians were not to be allowed to have their own houses or families lest their minds should get directed to preservation and extension of such property."

Plato builds up his Ideal State, as stated above, in three successive 'waves'. In the second wave he advocates the abolition of the family on the basis of communism of property and wives among the two upper classes to consolidate these classes into one family. In the entire theory of communism of both property and wives, the basic assumption is that much can be done to abolish spiritual evils by the removal of material evils and temptation, unity is a vital need of the state and demands a state regulated system of education and communism of property and wives in the ruling classes.

Plato believed that the highest life for the individual would be as a member of the state family and not of a private family. To Plato, communal life would not destroy the individuality of the guardian for individuality and community were not antithetic. Plato wanted to raise individuality to the highest spiritual level through his system of communism.

Of course, there is an essential difference in Plato's communism of property and of wives. In the case of property, there is common renunciation of property rather than common ownership by the guardians. In the case of wives and children, on the other hand, there is a definite system of communism in the sense of common ownership.

Plato wanted communism of property as union of political and economic power in the same hands is proved by universal experience to be fatal to political efficiency. He, therefore, gave monopoly of political power to the guardians and monopoly of economic power to the commercial class. The union of the two powers, *i.e.*, political and economic, would demoralise even his philosophers and degrade the state into a plutocracy.

Plato in The Republic analyses the successive corruptions of the Ideal state and traces them to a single source *i.e.* the union of political and economic powers. Such a union results in two things : (1) the holder of political power becomes avaricious, uses his position to amass wealth and ignores the path of wisdom; (2) the subjects resent his misappropriations and usurpation, murmur and revolt. Plato had firm faith that man, entrusted with the exceptional function of ruling, must be exceptionally equipped and must submit to exceptional regulations. That is why Plato's communism is to affect the upper classes only and not the whole community.

Plato's communism does not touch the third, *i.e.* the producing class which retains private property. His communism, therefore, does not affect the economic structure of society and allows the old individualistic system of production. The guardians are partners in renunciation and abnegation. They have no lands and no houses. They live in common barracks and have a common public mess. "Plato's communism has a touch of asceticism and medieval monasticism about it. It is aristocratic in conception and demands abnegation from only the best in the community. It is for, and not by, the whole community. It is political and not economic conception."

Platonic Communism Compared with Modern Communism

Plato's communism and modern communism have many similarities and dissimilarities.

Similarities. (1) Both systems believe that private property is sole source of all evils and so it should be abolished.

(2) Both believe in class struggle.

(3) Both favour governmental education of children exempted from parental care.

(4) Both regard art and literature only as a means to fortify the interests of the state.

(5) Both ignore the individuality of the citizens and based on a cast-iron dogma, a kind of state ethics and religion to which all individuals and social activities must be subordinated.

(6) Both are meant to promote political unity and social harmony and to develop the sense of social service.

(7) Both are calculated to eliminate unregulated economical competition based on individualism.

(8) Both believe in a small section of people as the most important and intelligent section of society.

(9) Both are based on the ignorance of the essentials of human nature and human instincts.

(10) Both are impracticable if applied on a vast scale.

Dissimilarities. (1) Plato's communism did not aim at the removal of property as an institution, whereas modern communism aims at the removal of private property as an institution.

(2) Plato's communism is rather half-communism. It is not an institution of the social whole.

(3) Platonic communism affects the ruling classes only and not the producers of economic goods; modern communism gives political power to economic, *i.e.* producing classes.

(4) Plato's communism is not based on the principle of equality, whereas modern communism is based on the principle of equality.

(5) Plato's communism involved abolition of private property as well as private family; modern communism affects private property only.

(6) Plato's communism means communism of wives also whereas modern communism does not touch the family.

(7) Plato's communism is to be attained through the agency of the state, whereas modern communism regards the state as an institution of exploitation in the hands of the capitalists. It is to be abolished root and branch.

(8) For Plato the state is all partnership in science, art, virtue and in all perfection, whereas modern communism is to be attained through the establishment of a classless society.

(9) Plato's communism establishes dictatorship of a philosopher-ruler, whereas modern communism advocates the dictatorship of the proletariat.

(10) Plato's communism is national in character and is achieved through an appeal to the altruism of the governing classes, whereas modern communism is international in character and is achieved through an appeal to the fidelity of the workers.

(11) Platonic communism is achieved through education and peaceful means, whereas modern communism believes in revolution and violent means for bringing the communist society into existence.

(12) Plato's communism is spiritualist whereas modern communism is all materialist.

Criticism. Plato's system of communism ignores the lower, *i.e.* producing classes, and does not represent a systematised whole. Unlike modern communism, it does not aim at the material well-being of the entire population of the state. It is negative in character, Meant only for the upper classes, it leaves the majority in the state untouched. As such, it clears the society into two groups and makes real unity in the state, its *raison d'etre* impossible.

Plato's advocacy of the abolition of private property (and private family) ignores the essential psychology of human action. It is a universal truth that one can best develop only with a certain minimum of personal property. Otherwise there is no incentive to work. It represses the instinct of acquisition and would lead to indolence. This doctrine is authoritarian and goes against human freedom and equality, kills diversity and leads to excessive centralisation. The richness of life depends not on unity and centralisation but in diversity based on private property and family. It does not touch the lower classes and is, at least, half communism. It ignores the producing class and slaves altogether and divides the society into groups of the proportioned and the propertyless. It is negative in character and does not aim at the material well-being of the society as does modern communism. This communism will create discontent among those who work much and get less.

Aristotle's Criticism. Aristotle severely and seriously criticises Plato's communism of property on the grounds that (1) real progress of society depends on cultivation of distinct interests by individuals based on private property; (2) there is a natural instinct and pride of ownership; (3) communism of property would destroy the sentiments of charity and benevolence; (4) unity of the state should be promoted by proper education and not by communism which only produces dead uniformity; (5) experience of life is against communism; (6) Plato's communism ignores the majority of the citizens and by dividing the state which two communities, renders unity and harmony impossible. Human selfishness leading to property and marriage cannot be eradicated by social legislation. Besides, property is a basis and natural extension of formality and an instruments of moral action. To Aristotle, Plato's communism represented a material cure for spiritual diseases. Common ownership and management, to Aristotle, will add to friction and disunity. Aristotle, however, was wrong in assuming that Plato had advocated a system of common possession, for Plato had provided for common use by guardians of a part the produce of land held by the agricultural class on private and individual basis.

Some writers opine that Plato's communism of property is irrational and ignores facts of history. The institution of property, they pointed out, is not more than four or five thousand years old. In primitive society, land and other things were held in common by the tribe or by the village community.

The sanctity of property is a modern notion. With the passage of time a change have taken place. Notions of private property are artificial and not natural or universal. They differ in different times and places and conditions of society. The right of private property is based on social expediency and is interfered with through taxation, death duties, super-tax and Laws of escheat and inheritance. It is rightly pointed out that if Plato's communism sacrificed the individual at the altar of the society, modern economic individual sacrifices the society in the interests of the individual.

Communism of Wives

For his guardians, Plato not only abolished private property but denied them family ties too. The family postulates property which is necessary for its existence. Renunciation of family ties, therefore, is an inevitable corollary of the renunciation of private property.

Plato found better and fitter support for his system of community of wives in current literature and Hellenic practice.

According to Herodotus, the Agathyrsians held their woman in common as also did the Libyan Nasomones and Asiatic Massagetes.

In Sparata women were lent out by their husbands to procreate children for the state.

Euripides, in his "The Protesilaus", advocated the community of wives.

To the Greeks, a wife was merely an instrument for the procreation of children.

Marriage was no sacrament to Plato — complete seclusion from man and affairs represented feminine excellence. He wanted to exalt the women and to enlist her in the service of the state, she must be taken out of her household drudgery and allowed a full and varied development of intellect and character. She must be reserved from ignorant servitude and granted intelligent independence.

To Plato the private home was the centre of selfish exclusiveness. Family selfishness may degenerate into family feuds, civic disorder and sedition. The family system and the family feeling were the primary cause of personal ambition and restricted loyalties and instituted against the spirit of *esprit de corps* in the community. Private family and private messing will not do for the guardians. Plato was convinced that not only a proper system of education but proper environment, based on community of wives and property, were necessary to produce, and maintain uncorrupted, his all important guardians. Hence, he advocated community of wives and property.

Women — Their Emancipation and Functions

Plato builds up his communism of wives on the basis of (1) the emancipation of women and (2) reform of marriage. In the boys of Plato, the public life in Greece was completely masculine. The city, for the most purposes, a Men's Club. The women confined themselves to home, bearing and rearing children. They were married at an early age of 15 and were regarded as a means for the protection of children. This, he considers, will encourage sedition and shelter selfishness in the state and will not allow its development. The day of emancipation of women will be the day of unity of the state, liberty to the individual and justice to both.

To him, the seclusion of women makes the state loss the services of half of the population. Plato wanted to exalt the women and to enlist her in the service of the State. She must be taken out of her household drudgery and allowed a full and varied development of intellect and character. For him, there is no difference of kind and capacity between man and woman as there is between man and woman. In matters of administration, nature makes no difference between the sexes, women will share with man a common education, a common responsibility for rearing children and common guardianship of the state in peace and war. Women can 'guard' the state just as bitches can hunt or shepherd a flock of sheep. Women are capable of holding civic or military offices and discharging their duties efficiently. "Let the age for holding office be in the case of a woman, forty, in that of a man, thirty years". "Let the age of military service be, for a man, from twenty to sixty but for a woman... after she has borne children, upto the age of fifty."

Plato assigns them some special functions in their peculiar province. They are to regulate marriages and the rearing of children. In the Laws besides priestesses, we read of a committee of women nurses who are to supervise married couple for the first ten years after marriage and report cases of obstinate misconduct. Nurses are required to care for and control children. Women nurses are to decide whether young widows are to marry or not. Ten of them, with ten "guardians of Law", form a court to allow divorce for incompatibility of temper. Later ages have, considerably, followed Plato in assigning women their place, in public life.

Regarding the reform of marriage, Plato would supersede monogamy at will by communism under state supervision in which wives and children of guardians will be common. According to him marriage was a "special solemn consecrated coupling with a view to bred for the public." The best among the men and women guardians must be united nuptially at proper age — 30 to 50 for men and 20 to 40 for women and during proper seasons in temporary marriages, and the offspring of these marriages must be reared in the state 'fold' or nursery. The number of these temporary marriages would depend upon the necessity of population in the city-state.

In the above system the parents will neither rear nor know their children and the children will regard as their parents all those who were brides and bridegrooms at a marriage festival a certain time before their birth. In this way the whole guardian class will become one family and will bound together by community of pleasure and pain and interests.

To him 'community of wives' did not mean socialisation or common enjoyments of sex life. The regulations for mating of guardians were severer than any imposed by injunction of religion. The extension of duty of guardians to both sexes clearly shows that sex life was to be lead occasionally and in the interests of the state only.

Plato advocated his communism of wives on three grounds *viz.*, political, moral and eugenic. He wanted to promote political unity in the state by converting the whole guardian class, males and females into one family. This would prevent a conflict between public duty and private interest and prevent civil discord. Morally, he wanted to create *esprit de corps* in the community by depriving individuals of private families and private interests and ambitions. The care of children and wife, necessity of amassing wealth for their support, pride of birth and devotion to family, divert men from pursuit of this idea and public duty. Under communism there will be no private family to compete with the state for an individual's loyalty and devotion. Absence of family will also promote brotherhood of man.

From the point of view of eugenics, he believed in the best only among the two sexes of guardians mating and rearing up a nation perfect in body and mind. Plato uses the analogy of animals to emphasise the point. He would 'expose' or destroy the weak babies. It was a scheme of eugenics to improve the national stock; it was one for the emancipation of women and for the nationalisation of the family and it was a scheme for promoting unity and solidarity in the state. Plato looked at the Communism of wives from the point of view of reason and of the state. The question of decency was one of environment and custom.

Plato, the First Feminist

During the days of Plato, a woman was merely an instrument for the procreation of children. As already mentioned, marriage to them was not a sacrament. Feminine excellence consisted in complete seclusion from men and public affairs. Plato was the first thinker who advocated emancipation of women, their exaltation and their enlistment in the service of the society. He was the first feminist. He insisted that women must be brought out of their household drudgery. They must be allowed a full and varied development of intellect and character. They must be rescued from ignorant servitude and granted intelligent independence.

Plato was convinced of the necessity, usefulness and feasibility of bringing women out into public life which would perfect the unity and strength of the state. Women and men were equal and had the same nature. There was no fundamental difference between man and woman as human entities. Women like men, had the three elements of Reason, Courage and Appetite, though in different degrees. They could perform the same functions as men did. The difference between men and women was one of *degree* and not of *kind.*

Plato held that "no practice or calling in the life of the city belongs to women as women or to men as men". In the field of administration and public service there is no difference between women and men. Women are capable of holding both civil and military offices. There must be equality between men and women of the guardians class in functions and in public status. Women must receive the same education as men.

Plato advocates the discouragement of polygamy and encouragement of monogamy in order to improve the lot of women. In the Laws, he suggests that those men who remain bachelors after 35 should be heavily taxed.

Plato is against excessive drinking which corrupts family life and brings misery to womenfolk. This opinion of Plato is very apt even today. Still womenfolk are suffering due to this evil practice of drinking by men.

In the case of emancipation of women Plato advocated beautiful ideas to secure their services for the society at large. As such, Plato was thinking more of their duties than of their rights. He stood for the equality of both sexes, so that both are enlisted in the service of the state. It must be realised also that his plea was for women of the guardian class only. For the women of the appetitive class, Plato had little to offer.

Some people opine that Plato's communism of wives is based on wrong notions. The difference between man and woman is not only one of sex and of degree but of kind. If women are characterised by gentleness, sensibility and mercy, men are energetic, strong and intelligent. These differences affect the whole nature of the individuals. Plato is wrong in assigning equality of capacity with men to women. There is no sentiment of imagination in Plato's sex relationship. His system banishes the all important sentiments of love, mercy and clarity germinating in the household. Even birds and beasts are faithful to excel other and protect their young ones.

However, we can say that Plato's communism was a heroic remedy for unsurmountable ills pervading the Greek society of those days. His approach was not totally idealistic. It was logical, practical and even pragmatic.

Criticism

Plato's views on family have also been widely criticised.

Plato emancipates women, only to condemn them to the masculine life of public duty, having nothing to do with domestic duties. Hard service of states does not suit the nature of women, their gentleness and grace.

By destroying the family, Plato destroys a time honoured institution and a tried school of morals. Private family is an institution of civilisation.

The Platonic system of community of wives ignores the influence of heredity, of family environment and traditions and of proper nature of the child.

Plato's system denies a child the gentle influence of the home, the sweetness of family affections and the loving devotion of members of the family.

Plato's system banished the sentiments of love, mercy and charity germinating in the family. Even birds and beasts are faithful to each other and protect their young ones.

Plato's system of state-controlled mating debased human beings to the position of prize-stock animals. It shows no human mercy to the weaklings, and idiots. It ignores human psychology and as such is unworkable. Moreover, it is impossible to produce a race of intellectual and physical giants by state-controlled mating.

Communism of wives is against the fundamental sex and paternal instincts and is unworkable. The sense of public duty cannot kill, except in a few abnormal cases, a racial and paternal instincts. Parentless children are likely to be poor specimens of humanity. To expect an individual to crush these instincts is to make too much of a demand on his devotion to the state.

Aristotle also criticises Plato's community of wives as he does with communism of property on the following grounds :

(1) It will create confusion and disharmony in the social order and will lead to pernicious polygamy.

(2) Unholy acts may be done against near relatives.

(3) The children, common to all, are bound to be neglected. Only a mother can rear a child properly.

(4) It is absurd to use the analogy of animals in support of community of wives.

(5) The state-controlled mating will be unworkable and will not bring the best males and females together.

(6) It will make the guardian class most unhappy.

(7) Household will also suffer if women are emancipated; but he forgets that Plato's communism leaves no separate household amongst guardians which may suffer.

(8) One female cannot be the wife of all guardians. If so, this will create disharmony instead of unity.

Plato underestimated the true significance of marriage. Truly, it is a question of life friendship and understanding but not merely cohabitation.

To Plato, the unity of state is to be secured property and family stand in the way; therefore the property and marriages must go. This is too sweeping. Again, he demands a degree of self-control that has never been realised among any large population.

By transforming the state into a family, Plato destroys the fundamental condition of the state, *i.e.,* self-sufficiency. The very nature of the state is plurality of dissimilarities which Plato's communism would destroy.

Assessment

However, Plato's communism cannot be condemned mercilessly. As regards practicability of the scheme, we should not forget that it was to be applied only to a small minority. Demand was made of the guardians in view of monopoly of political power given to them. Later even this vigour was diluted in the Laws. It is only the necessary consequence of his fundamental principles for the sake of which he made a clean sweep of all that stood in the way. His treatment is like that of a 'Doctrinaire' Radicalism in the phrase of Sabine. It means that he did not hesitate to destroy all the hindrances on the way to achievement of his ideal. He followed the argument where it led. Moreover, it is a great surprise to us that most of the modern problems like abortion, invalids and the bringing up of children were discussed by him in a most scientific manner. We are more nearer to the Greek world than to any part of the world's history. Hence, Catlin remarks, "Greek world is the microcosm of our macrocosm." Modern age considerably followed Plato in assigning women their place in public life. According to Taylor, Plato did not want to create an Utopia but he was fired with a passion for reforming the world.

7

Plato on Education

The concept of education occupies a prominent and predominant place in The Republic of Plato. It emerges from his philosophical thinking. It is intimately connected with his views on the nature of the state and the end which every free citizen should strive to attain. Justice is the life of breath of Plato's Ideal State and it could only be analysed through the instrument of education, rather state-regulated education. Herein lies the supreme importance of education in The Republic. Hence, the remark of Barker that "no representation but education is the key to Platonic education." In the phrase of Catlin, Plato "showed the courage of his conviction." He advocated his ideas about education with great force and vigour.

Education in Ancient Greece

Education, to the ancient Greeks, meant *worth* primarily. Worth was interpreted differently at different times and places in Hellas, always embodying, however, a sense of proportion, creating harmony between the various parts of the individual, between the individual and the society and between the individual and the Divine. Their individual excellence, embodying physical perfection and control over passions, was always subordinated to public usefulness because the state dominated the individual.

The aim of education, in the minds of both the Spartans and the Athenians — who, between themselves, represented the general character and educational ideals of the Greeks, but where mental attitudes were sometimes diametrically opposed to those of each other — being to perpetuate the modes of their national life, they used models in education which suited their own individual interests best.

The watchword of Spartan education was strength, both in the individual and the state. The Spartans adopted a vigorous system of military education and discipline. Even the Athenian Plato and Aristotle admired the organisation and efficient State control of the Spartan educational system which was divided into periods of individual's life *i.e.*, infancy, boyhood, youth and manhood.

At the age of seven, the State directly undertook at State expense, the education of the free boys. These boys lived in public barracks or boarding schools which was calculated to promote feelings of equality and sociability between the sons of the rich and the poor. Formal education consisted of gymnastics, music and choric dancing. Between the ages of 20 and 30, the course of study was little short of actual warfare. Discipline and endurance got easy precedence over intellectual excellence.

The Spartans were the true originators of the Boarding School system. Their boarding schools admitting only the free boys, were calculated to produce a particular type of character and mental outlook and a deep devotion for the Polis, its constitution and its law and institutions in the minds of the future rulers of Sparta.

Athens was for the fullest development of the individual, for his own as well as for social ends. She wanted to develop individual as well as public morality and wanted men not mere soldiers. Education was on individualistic lines and consisted of gymnastics and music. The Athenian conception of Music and much more catholic than that of Sparta. Out of Music grew up the liberal Arts. Originally Music covered music and poetry. To Socrates, philosophy was the "highest music," while by the time of Aristotle, Music had come to comprise grammar, rhetoric, dialectic, arithmetic, geometry, astronomy, drawing and music in the ordinary sense of the word. The Athenians attached greatest importance to music and poetry, the former representing a "daemonic power, capable of arousing or assuaging the passions" on which depended individual and social harmony, while the latter was in the beginning the vehicle of all literary expression.

At the age of seven, the Athenian boy attended two schools — of the music master and the physical trainer, *i.e.*, "gymnastics for the body and music for the soul." Till 15 the boys attended the schools. Higher Education was the privilege of the few. There was no religious education as such, nor had women any school education. The object of Athenian education was to build up character. Technical education was taboo in the schools, for the Athenians cared only for "perfection of body, extensive mental activity and culture and irreproachable taste."

Spartan Education and Athenian Education — A Comparison

(1) Education in Spartan was public, in Athens individualistic.

(2) In Sparta education was compulsory, utilitarian and for both sexes; that of Athens was mainly voluntary, humanistic and for boys.

(3) Sparta leaned towards gymnastics, Athens towards music.

(4) Sparta discouraged all but the poorest literary education, while Athens encouraged higher education through the medium of private schools run by sophists.

(5) The slaves had no place in the educational policy of either City-State.

Principles of Platonic Education

The essence of Platonic conception of education is the realisation of idea of 'Good'. It is intended for the enrichment of the soul and the broadening of the spirit. As Plato called it, is the 'one great thing' which will turn the 'inward eye' towards the 'inner light'. Plato believed that a state regulated education could create the spirit of devotion in a citizen and make him or her contribute his or her best to the State in one's own particular station in life. If the citizens are well educated, they will readily see through the difficulties and meet emergencies as they arise. Education was calculated to promote justice and to enable a man to fulfil his duty. Public education was therefore a direct corollary of Platonic justice. According to Barkar, Plato considered education as a means of social righteousness and realisation of truth and not of social success.

The real aim of education was to a man and woman socially, economically, intellectually and politically useful and fit. Plato believed in the perfectibility and plasticity of human nature. He placed his main reliance upon education, through which the ruler could mould the character of individual and train the citizens in unselfish devotion to duty and thereby to produce a harmonious state. In this manner, his theory of education meant to turn the state, in which there was nothing but injustice and lack of discipline, into a just state. For this reason he made education compulsory and state-controlled.

For Plato, education meant a great deal more than merely imparting information. It did not mean the storing up of external knowledge but the bringing of the soul into proper environment for its development. It involved the redirection of the whole personality, the turning of the eyes of soul towards the light which hitherto had been experienced. "There is a faculty residing in the soul of each person and an instrument enabling each of us to learn," so the redirection of the soul must be achieved by turning it towards the right object. The quality of the soul is to be imitative borrowed it with the right kind of environment and it will begin to assimilate itself. The main problem of education is to discover how to provide the individual in the midst of these things in whose likeness one wants it to grow. The aim of education is to enable the soul to see the beautiful and to good.

The soul being an imitative thing, is not passive but active. The function of education is not to put to ideas or knowledge into it; it is rather to draw out the best latent in it. Objects are not presented to the soul, but it moves towards them because it feels attracted towards them.

Since the soul reacts on its surroundings at all stages of its development, education in the matter of life time. Because it is a living and developing entity, it is affected by different agencies and media at various stages of its growth. During infancy and childhood, the soul is more susceptible to fancy imagination. The character is trained through emotions at this stage. Therefore, the aim of education during this period will be to stimulate the love of the beautiful in all its varied appearances.

During the age of adolescence and maturity when the reasoning powers begin to develop, the soul is reached through reasons. Here the education means the development of the understanding through science and philosophy. Thus, in youth, education would be love and acquisition of truth.

At the highest stage the purpose of education will be to bring the soul to a knowledge of the good, vision of the Absolute. In this stage, the education was to be general and vocational. Education must help the individual to discover his or her vocation in life.

Another future of Plato's theory of education is the true innovation he made upon the current Athenian practice. He is possibly the first feminist. He is for giving the same type of education to both boys and girls. Since he believed that there was no difference in kind between the native capacities of boys and girls. He felt that the state was being deprived of services of half of the population by denying the education and the rights of citizenship to women. He advocated their emancipation and equal education for them along with men. In his system, the women were to be eligible to the same office as men. Here he was one of the most modern and radical philosophers.

Plato's System of Education

Plato's plan of education represents a State controlled system of compulsory education for both sexes which is divided into two stages, called the elementary and higher education.

(1) *Elementary Education* : Upto the age of six, the imparting of instruction is not so important thing. The aim of education is not truth as a matter of fact but truth as a matter of principle. The child is to be taught first simple religious truth and then simple moral truth and insensibly to learn the lessons of good manners and good taste. A child must learn to properly hate and love things.

In early boyhood, till the age of eighteen, education is to be both physical and intellectual. Here is provided music for the soul and gymnastics for the body. At this stage, gymnastics includes all that is related to the care of the body. At this stage, Plato recommended music as it was through music, he held that the soul learnt harmony and rythm, and a disposition of justice. Music also moulds character and brings refinement of feeling. It preserves and restores health. It leads grace and health to the soul and body. At this stage there must be a study of the elements of the science. The real value of the study of sciences is two-fold : (i) They taught us to think and

(ii) in studying sciences the mind comes gradually to understand certain principles or forms of being which lead to the understanding of the good, Mathematics trains a mind to think clearly and precisely. The science of numbers was the mother of all sciences and arts. Plato's music consisted of purified poetry and literature generally, ordinary music and a study of dance. Thus, upto the age of eighteen there is to be general education in music, gymnastics and elementary sciences. From eighteen to twenty there is to be exclusive training in gymnastics, including military exercises, with the aim to develop courage and self-control, character and discipline. At the age of twenty men without good intellectual capacity will drop off as the result of public test.

(2) *Higher Education* : Higher education extends from the age of twenty to thirtyfive. An elimination test (public test) will take place at the age of twenty years and less talented will drop off and the more promising will undergo another course of education lasting for ten years. Higher education is meant for members of both the sexes selected to be members of the two ruling classes.

The period of fifteen years is further divided into the parts from twenty to thirty and from thirty to thirtyfive. In the first part men and women are to be given systematic scientific education. At this stage education is both intellectual and physical. Natural and mathematical sciences are to be taught. Stress is laid on mathematics, including arithmetic, plane and solid geometry, astronomy, logic and the development of dialactic power. There would also be training in public service, particularly military service.

At thirty, a second selective test will be held. The less gifted are weeded out as auxiliaries or subordinate officers of the state. The more gifted are given further training in the science of dialectics. They are given positions of authority in the state. This lasts for 15 years. At fifty, the selected for approved would study the good itself. They are to govern and organise the state. They will be the supreme council in the state dividing their time between theoretical study of the good and practical governments.

Plato's system of education has little place for vocational and technical education. The system was essentially one for leadership. Leaders must have knowledge, experience, character, courage and self-control. They must have intelligence, knowledge and insight. The Platonic system had a psychological basis and was progressive in character. It meets the demands of the soul. It was an education for all-round development.

Criticism

(1) Plato's scheme of education, portrayed in The Republic, is meant for the guardians only. He ignores education for the artisans. According to his conception of justice, every one must, as efficiently as can, perform his allotted duty in the state. But Plato's education would train the guardians

only for their duties. Taylor criticises that it is confined mainly to particular class and knowledge of such becomes the monopoly of the guardians. Thus, the system shows an aristocratic contempt or anti-democratic character. Salime also criticises his conception of education in this respect. Moreover, this system is unjust and arbitrary to the producing class. It is simply meant for the rulers and administrators.

(2) The whole emphasis in the system is on selecting guardians of the state. It raises the question whether the state produces guardians or *vice versa*. Further, it is the end in view simply the development of this small aristocracy of talents or the well being of the whole.

(3) Plato's system of education minimises the influence of literature and exaggerates that of mathematics on mind. His type of education will produce an ideal philosopher, not an ideal men of action, and therefore will suit the very few not the many.

(4) Plato has got a very poor idea of art. It is because he thinks that music and poetry are harmful if they do not serve the interest of the state. So he advocated the censorship of the state on art.

(5) Plato's system of education aims at the happiness of the whole but not of individuals.

(6) His education is designed to create an ideal philosopher more than an ideal man of action, who will decide quickly than execute. The utility of such rulers is doubtful.

(7) The system is designed to produce citizens of a particular pattern. Each man is universe by himself. So to think in terms of giving a straight jacket of education is not all a healthy approach. It will not admit of sufficient diversity of intellectual development which alone can tune up the character of society. Plato does not realise that education should be relative to the individual. That is why Plato has been characterised as fascist by some writers.

(8) At many places Plato brings in the analogy of physicians to justify his training to the guardians, which is inappropriate.

(9) It encourages simply expert knowledge, which is sometimes abominable as evident in G.B. Shaw's Doctor's Dilemma.

(10) Jowett sees two paradoxes in Plato's scheme of education *viz.*, the extraordinary use of music and the absolute control of the soul over the body. But if music excites popular emotions, it has powerful influence for good too.

(11) There is no definiteness in his education about the due place that should be recorded to action and contemplation. Sometimes the goal of education is the Idea of the Good and sometimes it is social service.

(12) This process of education, extending to 35 years of age, will not only be expensive, but also would kill initiative in men till that age. The scheme is, in this respect, self-defeating.

(13) Plato's scheme of education, like his communism condemns his guardians to a life of military monasticism.

Despite this criticism, Platonic education stands in his Republic as a 'Polar Star' which has guided many a philosopher who followed him. It anticipated many modern theories of education. It goes without saying that its aim of spiritual uplift of the individual is strikingly similar to that of the modern liberal education. Secondly, one cannot totally ignore the context of the times in which Plato wrote. What all he attempted was a reform of the haphazard education that prevailed in Greece in those times. Hence, the remark of Salime that his principles of education were running commentary on the existing system of education. Moreover, the place occupied by education in his political philosophy brings home the truth that a good education is the foundation for any good state.

8

Plato on Functional Specialization

Plato's Ideal State is built on his conception of functional specialization. The Platonic Doctrine of Specialization took its due from the Socratic view that expert knowledge was necessary for the conduct of public affairs. The professional soldier and the professional orator had already appeared in the days of Plato and had forcefully pointed to the virtue and efficacy of specialization. Besides, a certain amateurish meddlesomeness of the untrained demos in Athens drove home to Plato the need of specialization. The Athenian democracy in which the ignorant encroached on the sphere of the expert and in which everybody felt entitled to do as he pleased was the exact opposite of Plato's conception of an Ideal State based on functional specialization according to nature and aptitude and in which the direction of the state was assigned to a specially bred and trained class of guardians. The Spartans deliberately bred for military efficiency. Plato admired efficiency but wanted to eliminate the danger of Spartan dullness and uniformity by insisting on functional specialization based on different kinds and degree of nature, aptitude and intelligence.

Plato's theory of functional specialization was based on his conception of the reciprocal needs of human beings and the necessity of division of labour. Societies arise out of the needs of man. The wants of the individuals of a community are multifarious. Everybody, by himself, cannot meet all his wants for lack of time and capacity. "We are not born each perfectly alike but differing in disposition — one fitted for doing one thing, and another for another... ." Everybody must have a certain minimum for food, clothing and housing arrangement, *etc*. To satisfy these minimum requirements, a large number of commodities is required which is, ordinarily, beyond the capacity of an individual to prepare for himself. This gives rise to a desire for the necessity of co-operation between individuals. People come together and form an economic union for the satisfaction of human needs. But they are quick to learn the advantages of specialization.

According to Plato, "All things are produced more plentifully and easily and of a better quality when one man does one thing which is natural to him and does it at the right time and leaves other things." This principle of one man one work, according to nature, leads to division of labour, satisfaction of mutual needs and exchange of services. In fact a proper exchange of services demands a proper division of labour and specialization of functions based not on instinct as among ants and animals but on purposive direction and virtue of justice. This conception of Plato differs from a view of society where social relation are based on contact and agreement born of free choice.

The theory of functional specialization of Plato flowed directly from his conception of justice, according to which an individual performed efficiently that task for the society for which he was best fitted. Society is conceived by Plato as a system of services in which every member both gives and receives. An ideal state would properly arrange the most adequate satisfaction of needs and the most harmonious exchange of services. Nature endows a man with the capacity and privilege of free will and action but the freedom which the state secures and guarantees him is not so much for the exercise of his free will as for the performance of the social task allotted to him leading to interchange of services within the society.

For the necessity and usefulness of specialization of functions, Plato divides his ideal polity into three classes : the guardians, the auxiliaries, *i.e.*, administrations and fighters, and artisans and farmers. Each of these three has its appointed function in the state and each of these concentrates itself entirely on the discharge of that function. Economic sustenance, defence and government, the three necessary and main functions of the state are converted into professions and assigned to professional classes by Plato. The state originated because of the necessity of efficient and, therefore, specialised co-operation and functional specialisation in the state took its cue from the three human faculties of appetite, spirit and reason creating the three professional classes of workers, soldiers and philosopher-rulers. Plato's classification of society resembles the Pythagorean as also contemporary Egyptian division of society into three classes. Functional specialization began in the economic sphere, proved its worth there and was extended to other classes. If specialization improved the art and capacity of a cobbler it was the more essential for a perfect soldier and a guardian.

The functional specialization led to the much desired unification of the state. According to Plato, "If a separate class of well-bred and trained specialists were appointed to the task of government, there would hardly be either incentive or room for the old struggle to capture the reins of government which characterized the Athens of his day. If each class of professionals kept within its own boundary, there would be no inter-class conflicts and no social and political disorders in the state. Selfishness would disappear and unity pervade the state, for selfishness consists essentially in going outside one's own sphere. Functional specialization would promote peace, efficiency, and unity in the state by eliminating unnecessary and unlimited competition in every sphere. The intention was that... each individual should always be put to the use for which nature intended him, one to one work, and then every man would do his own business, and be one and not many, and so the whole city would be one and not many."

Plato's Division of Classes

Plato divided the state into three classes on the basis of functional specialization. The third and lowest class of Plato contained not only the wage-earning or health-producing artisans and farmers but also many civilians, independently of their economic status. The division of society in the Ideal State, therefore, was not on economic basis but on that of different types of service rendered. But then the upper two classes having been debarred from the possession of private property, it was true that the lowest class, containing wage-earners, professional artisans and employers of labour was left all the wealth of the state in its hands and was, therefore, economically, too, distinguishable from the upper two classes.

Plato's Class-State

Plato's class-state, with its three classes of rulers, soldiers and producers, is based on the double principle of division of functions and capacity for virtue. Members of producing class perform different functions but are mutually equal. They are all men of inferior virtues. This equality they do not hold with members of the guardian class, who are superior to members of the producing class in virtue to the soldiers. Plato's Ideal State is a class-state with the upper class guardians. Plato believed in the definite in the definite inequality of men from the standpoint of attainment of virtue and held that it was to the advantage of producing class men to submit to the guidance and control of guardians who represented virtue and wisdom.

The social structure, based on functional specialization in the Ideal State portrayed in The Republic, has been described as a system of castes, the third class including the modern working class or the industrial labour. Really, there is no system of castes in The Republic. A 'caste' man is born into it and cannot get out of it. It is true that Plato believed in the powerful intellectual and moral influence of heredity and environment which gave a man his natural place into 'class' from which he sprang, particularly as he advocated the rearing of children under careful eugenic regulations. But the 'classes' of Plato were not exclusive. Individuals of various classes were to be subjected, in their early life, to repeated tests of intelligence and character and were to be promoted or demoted to higher or lower classes according to their natural endowments and abilities. Career was left open to ability and character. "Some of you have the power of command, and in the composition of these he has mingled gold, wherefore also they have the greatest honour; others he has made of silver, to be auxiliaries; others again, who are to be husbandmen and craftsmen. He was composed of brass and iron and the species will generally be preserved in the children. But as all are of the same original stock, a golden parent will sometimes have a silver son, or a silver parent a golden son." This quotation from The Republic rules out the charge of caste rigidity in Plato's social system. Plato's highest class is of philosophers, not a servile class. Property is confined not to the upper classes but to the lowest.

In the Laws, Plato abandons the three-fold division into classes and recommends only two groups, *i.e.*, (1) free men excluded from trade and industry and (2) industrials. The population is also grouped into four classes according to property held.

Evils of the System

Plato commended the division of the state into three classes on the basis of functional specialization to promote unity and efficiency in the state. Specialization does conduce to efficiency and speed and is a good thing but in his love of specialization of function, Plato did not pay proper heed to the following :

Plato did not sufficiently realise the wholeness of human being. The personality of a man is a complex whole and is not capable of rigid divisions into watertight compartments. Most men are endowed with all the three faculties of appetite, courage and reason, it being merely a question of the predominance of one of these faculties over the other two. They want to exercise all these faculties. In every individual, reason supplies the rule of action, spirit supplies energy and appetite the necessary stimulus for action. If every individual were condemned to the narrow limits of performing one function only, he could not develop his personality and realise the fullness of his life. The consequent loss is not only personal but that of the whole community. Plato conceives of the unity of human soul resulting not from the reconciliation of the three elements in the soul but from the subjugation of two by the third. The same applies to his Ideal State which means both excessive separation of classes and excessive unification.

Functional specialization makes one sacrifice the all-round view of the amateur for the specialised knowledge of the professional. What ought to be aimed at is the combination of the viewpoints of the amateur and the expert which is impossible under the Platonic state-system and which makes the British Constitution of today the best of many good constitutions.

The Platonic system of functional specialization would tend to divide the state into so many expert bureaus and the system itself would degenerate into a bureaucratic system with all its concomitant evils.

In the Platoic system of specialization of functions, the governmental powers are given to one class of people, the guardians only. This means that the state, at its highest level, becomes identical with a single section of the community, the philosophers. Now, if political power is to be definitely assigned to the philosophers, to exclusion of all other classes in the state, the ruling class is bound, human nature being what it is, sooner or later, to identify the public interests with its own class interests. You can seldom have a purely disinterested altruistic class of people to govern a state for a long time. The identification of class is sure to create resentment and discontentment in the state, resulting in disorder, anarchy, political revolution and the overthrow of the whole system of government.

The largest measure of common good, in a state, can only be brought about by the co-operation of the largest number of people making their mental and physical contributions for the general welfare. This would not be possible under the Platonic state system based on rigid specialization.

Plato's system of functional specialization and his suggestions to bring this about concentrate on the guardian class. His system comparatively ignores the remaining mass of the population in the state and is, therefore, lop-sided. Moreover, his philosopher-rulers, "spectators of all time and all existence" and contemplators of the highest Good, are likely to show that lack of political realism which comes of active contact with and participation in every phase of public life and activity.

9

Decline of the Ideal State

In his famous book Republic Plato deals about Philosophy of history (Books VIII and IX). In these two books, he tries to explain the cause and follow the course of the decline of the Ideal State.

In dealing with the decline of the Ideal State, Plato emphasises that the State is a product of social mind which itself is based on the mind of the individual, *i.e.,* on human psychology. He, therefore, deals with the decline of the human soul and, therefore, of human society. This decline is due to disorganisation in the functioning of the human soul and the various elements of society. The Ideal State or society begins to decline when different organs or elements of society tend more and more to perform wrong functions.

Plato's Ideal State is ideal because it is based on a certain principle of justice. The degree of decline of the Ideal State depends upon the degree of disturbance of this adjustment and the potency of the causes which bring about this disturbance and deterioration. Every State has its basic principle and the corruption of this principle brings about a corresponding corruption or decline of such a state.

The relationship between the decline of the individual and that of the society established by Plato is very clear from his Republic. One of the main causes of decline in society and the State is division and faction among its rulers. Human society also declines if it fails to understand and act on the principles of its own life.

Another important cause of the decline of a society is excess and the reaction in the opposite direction generated by excess.

Each perverted society, *i.e.,* oligarchy, democracy or tyranny, pursues its basic object to the extreme and creates disturbances within itself. Oligarchy is ruined by excessive pursuit of wealth, democracy by excessive freedom and equality.

In its decline the Ideal State passes through a number of stages. In its first corruption, the Ideal State takes the form of Timocracy in which Reason, *i.e.,* Philosophy loses its pre-eminence and regulative influence and gives the price of position of spirit. The basic principle of Timocracy is Honour and high spirit. This points to ambition and war.

A Timocracy is essentially a military state, like that of Sparta in the days of Plato. Justice of the society is beginning to disappear and with it the balance, harmony and unity of the society. Soldier has replaced the philosopher and honour has taken the place of reason.

The second stage in the decline of the society begins when aptitude dominates it and controls both reason and spirit and the end of the state becomes the pursuit and satisfaction of material wants. Timocracy as a mix constitution, already contained the appetitive, *i.e.* oligarchic element in it. The appetitive element now becomes the regulative principle of society which now becomes oligarchy which represents the second corruption or the ideal society. The principle of justice in the society receives a severe jolt.

In oligarchy, the principle of justice is ignored. Government is based now not on functional capacity and merit but on possession of wealth and property. Wealth is pursued for its own sake. This gives rise to economic individualism, selfishness and spirit of faction. Officers are awarded irrespective of merit or training. Pursuit of wealth divided the society into the rich and the poor. There is development of class consciousness. Division and disunity in society become apparent.

As a result of this oligarchy degenerates into Democracy which represents the third corruption of the ideal State. The basic principle of Democracy is Appetite purchased on the basis of perfect liberty and equality. In democracy all feel equally entitled to all the officers of the State irrespective of merit. To Plato, Democracy was no better than monarchy. Democratic liberty was license. It was lack of self-control and social responsibility. With its excessive emphasis on liberty and equality, democracy was polyarchic and creates many States within a State. Ultimately, its own excesses bring it down. There is a struggle for mastery in a democracy between the appetitive equalitarian and libertarian elements with the result that it is overthrown by tyrant.

The last stage in the decline of the society is reached when the most unscrupulous assume absolute control of the State *i.e.,* tyranny. It is antithesis of the unselfish rule of philosophy in the Ideal State. The basic principle of "tyranny is, brutal and lawless appetite to the last of the flesh and the pride of power."

Plato tried to visualise the course of degeneration of the Ideal State as against the historical side of the question.

Plato wanted to portray non-ideal forms of State such as Timocracy, Oligarchy, Democracy and Tyranny and thereby provide a basis of comparison with the actual and historical States.

Aristotle criticises the Platonic picture of the decline of the Ideal State from the historical point of view. He asserts that the society in the transformation and degeneration does not follow the course and sequence laid down by Plato.

Oligarchy does not always result in democracy or democracy in tyranny. A democracy may be succeeded by an oligarchy or by a tyranny.

Hence, it must be realised, however, that whereas Plato was concerned with the philosophy of history and wrote essentially on *a priori* basis. Aristotle was generalising on the actual history of his own day.

Thus, Plato in his Republic gives a clear picture of the decline of the Ideal State.

10
Elements of Individualism in Plato

Plato has given a beautiful sketch about the elements of Individualism in his book.

Plato is said to be the first communist and the first totalitarian thinker but his theory of the state is not without traces of individualism about it. His collectivism was less a result, of direct thinking than a reaction to the rabid individualism about it. His collectivism was less a result of direct thinking than a reaction to the rabid individualism prevalent in the Athens of his day. For this extreme individualisms which destroyed the harmony of civic life in Athens, Sophists as a class of professional teachers were, to a very considerable extent responsible. In the teachings of the Sophists may be traced a tendency to apotheosize the 'atomic' individual. To Protagoras, a leading Sophist, "Man is the measure of all things." Things exist and are, as they are, according to their determination or measurement by the individual as such. Things are for every individual as they seem to him. This doctrine, translated into the moral sphere, would justify an individual code of ethics and politics. It would ethicise private individual standard of morality and make every individual the determinant and judge of what is right or wrong.

True, Protagoras was not a rank individualist and exhorted people to participate equally in justice and reverence and lead a common civic and political life which could not be done without certain common social standards of action but his dictum of man being the measure of all things was developed by other Sophists in the direction of extreme individualism.

Another great Sophist, Antiphon, lent his weight on the side of excessive individualism and took up a position more or less analogous to that of Thrasymachus in the Republic of Plato. To Antiphon, law-abindingess is bad for, on the whole, it fails the test of test either ethics or expediency.

Coercive law, to Antiphon, often runs counter to the natural law of life. Evidently in taking up this view of things, Antiphon and his fellow Sophists follow a line of abstract individualism divorced from the actualities of life. They conceive of an individual as an isolated unit, not as a social being; civic laws must be useful to the individual. Laws, for instance, enforcing respect for and rights in property are of advantage of all individuals. Sophistic individualism led to the contractual, as opposed to the organic, theory of the state.

If Sophism, on the whole, led to atomic individualism, Plato believed in social individuality. In the Republic — the most important and most representative of his dialogues — Plato sets to himself the task of finding the location and nature of justice which he finds in each individual discovering his true vocation in his life and excelling in it by confining himself to it. Even though Plato is emphasizing the social excellence of the individual, yet the individual is not out of his mind. A man must discover the type of work for which nature has endowed him best from moral, intellectual and physical points of view and must concentrate on it. This concentration will not, to Plato, destroy the personality of the individual but will enrich it. Instead of being jack of all trades, an individual should be master of one and through it of himself. That Plato does not ignore the individual will himself expand and he will secure the common interest along with his own. Plato realised that the greatest advantage to the individual accrued from his concentration on and excelling in one vocation in life to the exclusion of others. The greatest and best expansion of his personality lay in the development of those faculties with which Nature had already endowed him.

Plato does not sacrifice the individual, as such, to the State. It is the microscopic minority of the guardians whom he makes merge themselves in the state. He does not call upon the mass of the community belonging to the producing classes to efface themselves for the good of the State. In fact it is for the good of this mass that he would sacrifice the guardians who stand for the State. He thus conceives of the subjects to be identical with the good of the State. He demands sacrifice of the ruler and not of the ruled.

How far does Plato's system of communism destroy individualism and is anti-individualistic? For one thing, we must realise that his communism does not affect the overwhelming majority of the society, *i.e.*, the appetitive or producing classes. Plato leaves untouched the individualistic system of production. His communism and collectivism affect the small guardian class. Does it destroy the individuallity rights or freedom of members of the guardian class? He is certainly against false notions of atomic individualism, natural inherent right and freedom which permitted a man to do as he liked. To Plato, an individual is not an isolated unit. He is a part of the whole, *viz.*, the society, and has his definite place in the whole. He has his part to play in the social whole. His individuality, rights or freedom have meaning in so far as they contribute to his playing this part freely and nobly. An individual is entitled to freedom and rights which might secure him the conditions in which he can play his social part worthily. Plato's communism is meant to secure for the individual 'freedom' from every entanglement which might stand in the way of his following his true vocation in life and thereby enriching the society and his own personality. The personality of the individual is most cramped when the individual stands by himself. It broadens and expands when the individual functions as a part in a social whole. Plato is quite true in asserting that the individual is narrowest when he stands by himself. But is not the personality of an individual a sum-total of his interests? Does not the Platonic formula of 'one man, one work' drastically cut down the interests of the individual and thereby dwarf his personality? To an argument of this type a Platonist would reply that it is not the diffusion of interests but intensity of interest that matters and which enriches the personality of the individual. It is this interest which Plato's conception of justice aimed at and which led to true individualism.

Plato's attitude towards democracy represents another illustration of his hatred of false individualism and its concomitants of absolute liberty and equality of all individuals. Plato was against democracy which dispensed equality alike to the equal and a the unequal. Equality, to Plato, in its true sense, should mean not equal rights for equal capacities. Nature endowed different people differently. This different in natural endowment as also in environment created different capacities in different individuals. Though Plato stressed natural inequality between individuals and was against equal rights to all, as a true individualist he was prepared to concede equal opportunities to all. This is well borne out by his system of education which bears unmistakable signs of individualism about it. In this system of education, Plato has combined principles of equality of opportunity and of essential inequality of individuals. Up to the age of 20, he gives the same education to all, male or females, and creates uniformity of conditions and equality of opportunities for all. At the age of 20, he lays down a test to weed out the less endowed from the more fortunate ones. The latter are given another course of training for another 10 years after which there is another weeding out test.

Realising that every individual is endowed by nature differently from other, Plato calls upon the individuality to discover his true vocation in life and find his true individuality by specialising in that vocation. Plato was against individualism based on false democratic egalitarianism and false notions of individual freedom. False freedom was destructive of the society and of the individual. A man with a false sense of freedom puts his hands at everything but is good at nothing. He has no powers of concentration and self-discipline which are necessary for the real development of his personality.

The later works of Plato are more individualistic than his Republic. With ripening age, Plato tones down his early collectivism. In the Laws, Plato gave recognition to the personality of the individual more than the communism of Republic permitted. He allows the holding of property by the guardians. After Plato, Greek political theory became undoubtedly more individualistic. Aristotle abhorred Plato's communism. True, to Aristotle, a man who lived outside the Polis was either a bast or a god, *i.e.*, he found his true individuality only in the State. But Aristotle believed in individual self-sufficiency, not of an isolated self but of a social unit. In order to attain self-sufficiency, a man develops into a citizen. Post-Aristotelian political thought in Greece became pronouncedly individualistic. The Cynic, Cyrenaics and other Schools of Thought made individualism the basis of their systems. To them, the individual must be sufficient unto himself. The individual must pursue his good and his happiness irrespective of society. The State and the society were not needed to supply any norms of action for the individual. Every individual represented his own norm of conduct.

11

Plato and The Idea of The Good

In his 'Republic' Plato tries to analyse the nature of 'Good' in a beautiful manner. He says that to some 'good' is wisdom, to others it is pleasure. He also says that there are bad pleasures which cannot be 'good'. To Plato, 'good' "meant unity in which all time and all existence were gathered up. It was the truth of all things, and also the light in which they shone forth and became evident to intelligence, human and divine. It was the cause of all things, the power by which they were brought into being. It was the universal reason diverted of a human personality. It was the life as well as the light of the world, all knowledge and all power were comprehended in it. The way to it was through the mathematical sciences, and these too were dependent on it".

Jowett paraphrases Plato's idea of good in a graphic manner. According to him Plato's idea of the good means "intelligent principle of law and order in the universe, embracing equally man and nature." "Viewed objectively, the idea of the good is a power or cause which makes the world without correspond with the world within." In the world of human knowledge the idea of the good is the most difficult to comprehend and realise, but when realised it becomes the cause of all that is right and beautiful in all things, illuminating the visible world and giving truth and reason.

According to Plato that a 'perfect' ruler must be a philosopher, for he only knows the Idea or essence of Justice and of Beauty and of Temperance, in order that he may fashion into their likeness, the lives and characters of those whom he rules. He must ultimately, know the 'Idea' of which all these ideas of Justice, Beauty and Temperance are but phases and from which alone springs the Idea of the Good. The Philosopher-ruler must know the purpose of all doing and all-being. He must know the end of all human existence in order to be able to do the work allotted to him in the schemes of things in a way which might subserve that end.

There is an ultimate purpose both in the action and the thought of human mind and in the existence of the world in which mind acts and which mind comprehends according to Plato. Action, knowledge and existence all imply the Idea of the Good; right action is action in the light of the knowledge that the Good is the reason of all existence. Right education culminates in the knowledge of the Idea of the Good. Education is very essential. It, therefore, issues in doing as well as knowing. Virtue is knowledge. All action is directed by knowledge.

To Plato, the Idea of the Good is not merely an abstract conception, nor is it identical with any particular existing object; it reveals itself in everything that truly exists. It is the source of all truth, of knowledge, of beauty and of moral goodness. Its apprehension by the soul is knowledge its dwelling in the soul is virtue, its shining forth to the soul — through the medium of sense — is beauty. Its manifestation in the State is Justice.

The Idea of the Good may be comprehended by Reason but its nature can only be described by an analogy. As the sun illumines the sensible world and is the source of the eye's power of vision and of nourishment and growth in all things, to the Idea of the Good illumines the intelligible world, gives the objects of knowledge their true being and gives the soul power to know and to grow in knowledge and in virtue. It is the sources of all knowledge as also the highest object of knowledge. The Idea of the Good throws light on and gives validity to every form of knowledge.

For Plato the Idea of the Good was an object of mystical faith rather than of rational intuition. Plato does not claim to know much about it. His commentators have interpreted it in various ways. It means unity in which all time and all existence are gathered up. It is the Truth of all things and also the light which illumines them. It is the cause of all things and the Power which has brought them into existence. It is the universal Reason. It is the life as well as the light of the world. All knowledge and all power are comprehended in it. The way to it, according to Plato, is through mathematical science; ideas of number, order, harmony and development enter into it.

All men wanted to attain happiness according to Plato. That happiness should be attained through the success of their lives. This happiness and success came out of and were identifiable with 'Goodness'. A 'good' man is one who "conducts his own affairs, those of his household, those of the city well." Through success in life, in the best sense of the word, is to possess "good", Material things are 'good' only when we know to use them. There is nothing intrinsically 'good' in them. A flute is good to a man who knows how to use it. Material things are 'good' if their user is 'good'. It is the soul of a man which uses his body and his material possessions. To be 'good', a man's soul must be good and healthy condition. The goodness of the soul is the wisdom. It enables him to use his body and of his possessions in a right way. To attain wisdom, a man must 'know himself'.

To Plato 'goodness' is essential not only to the individual but also to the state because 'goodness' is embodied in the art of Government or in political wisdom. That is why Plato, in the Republic, lays down a very rigorous course of education for all his important guardians who with their knowledge of the Good will create a 'good' or 'perfect' State.

Socrates believes that truth though the same for all, yet lived in the minds of individual men. Plato conceives of truth in the form of abstract, self-existant ideas, knowable only by an exceptionally endowed few. This is why Plato, in his scheme of education and ideal polity ignores the masses.

Willoughby points out his mistake, consists in exalting the universal into "transcendental entity instead of an immanent principle."

Plato's belief that virtue was knowledge led to the further conclusion that there is objectively a good life, both for societies and individuals, which may be the subject of methodical intellectual definition and speculation.

Plato thus in the Idea of the Good clearly indicates and vindicates the essentiality and necessity of goodness and knowledge both for societies and individuals in the State.

12

Plato on Democracy

The age of Pericles is considered as the 'Golden Age' in the history of Greece. So also this age of Pericles in Athens was the hey-day of Greek democracy.

During this period Athenian democracy was based on the twin notion of government of the city-state by the people and the development of individual. There existed direct democracy. It managed the internal and external affairs of the city-state of Athens without the usual cabinet of ministers.

The sovereign body of Athens was the Popular Assembly which controlled the Council. The Assembly made peace and war, appointed generals and gave audience to foreign ambassadors. Legal equality prevailed there. It was during this period that Hellas reached its spiritual and intellectual heights and made wonderful contribution to the civilisation of mankind. This period brought about an equation between the citizen and the city.

During this period every citizen took interest in public affairs in Athens. As Pericles said in his funeral speech, "We alone regard a man who takes no interest in public affairs not as a harmless but as a useless character, and we Athenians are able to judge..."

Greek democracy has given us a wonderful start in Philosophy, Letters, Sculpture and Painting and which has systematised Science and Arts for us. Periclean democracy gave us the standards to judge modern institutions and civilisation. It gave us the idea of law and government and of equality and liberty. It has given us the spirit of self-criticism and self-improvement.

Whatever the actual form of Government, ultimate power lay with the mass of the citizens. There was a common divine worship at public cost and the gods of the city-state were the gods of the individual citizens. The individual formed an integral part of the city-state.

To the Greeks, citizenship meant the capacity to rule and be ruled in turn. Slaves and workmen were denied the rights and responsibilities of citizenship and took no part in the government of the city-state. Greek democracy functioned well because every Greek had a deep and abiding reverence for the city-state and its 'laws'. The equality of all in the eyes of law promoted individual freedom.

In the course of time, Athenian democracy degenerated into mobocracy. Justice became the interest of the stronger and this paved the way for the tyrant. Greek democracy now became tainted with irresponsible individualism, particularism, want of self-restraint, personal ambition and the spirit of faction. Human nature, war, passion, faction and hunger created a painful impression on Plato and Aristotle.

Plato on Democracy

Plato came of a family which was highly critical of democracy. He saw the growing ruin of Athens under democracy and was horrified to witness the death of Socrates at the hands of the Athenian Demos. He refers to democracy in his 'Republic' as "a charming form of Government, full of variety and disorder." Again, he writes that "the laws of democracy remain a dead letter; its freedom is anarchy; its equality the equality of unequals." He discredits the views of Herodotus and Thuchydides on democracy. Democracy is for Plato a state of civic dissolution in which everyone follows his own inclination and pursuit. It is lawless and disorderly. According to Plato, in democracy even horses and asses claim all the rights and dignities of free citizen.

According to Plato a cyclic change in the form of Government is inevitable. It follows the order of monarchy, timocracy, oligarchy, democracy and tyranny. Democracy violates the first principle of society, equality and equal rights for equal capacities are emphasised. It does not care about the proper education and the training of the statesmen.

Plato classifies government in the Politicus on the following basis :

(1) Number of those holding political power and

(2) Relation of government to law, into monarchy, aristocracy and democracy which are subject to law, and tyranny, oligarchy and democracy which are not subject to law.

Plato holds that democracy is the worst form of Governments which are subject to law but the best of those which are not subject to law.

To him, political power must be based on broadest culture. His first preference is a philosopher-king; his second an aristocracy of intellect. He has no patience for the democratic idea of government by the uninitiated and uninstructed masses. The Ideal State of Plato, built on the idea of ideocracy, rules out democracy.

As mentioned earlier *i.e.*, in previous chapters, justice was the corner-stone of the Platonic state, and justice was knowledge in action. An ignorant Demos did not have the insight, education and excellence of character to promote justice in the state unlike philosopher-king.

Though Plato disliked democracy, he never failed to recognise the merits of democracy. In democracy people have an equal share of freedom and equal opportunities for power. A democratic state represents the greatest variety of human nature.

Criticism

(1) Plato in his denunciation of democracy, and exaltation of ideocracy, forgot that the rule of the Philosopher-king or of the aristocracy of the intellect could not last long. The choice, then, has to be made between oligarchy and democracy.

(2) It is a pity that Plato failed properly to appreciate the many virtues of democracy.

(3) Plato minimised the importance of the civic education of the citizens coming from participation in governmental work.

(4) Plato failed to realise, what Pericles and Aristotle did, that Demos as a rule, shows sound commonsense.

In spite of all faults, democracy allows the widest possible extension of liberty and equality.

Aristotle on Democracy

Aristotle holds that two principles are characteristic of democracy, *viz.* freedom and the government of the majority. A democrat wants to live as he likes and enjoy freedom.

Aristotle was against equalitarian democracy for he believed in equality among those who possessed equal virtue which was confined to the leisured citizen body comparable to the two guardian classes of Plato. Only leisured classes could take part in democracy. According to him leisure does not mean worklessness or recreation. It represents intense activity on the part of citizens to good life.

To Aristotle, a democracy, is one in which the supreme power is in the hands of the freemen. This rules out the slaves from any share in the government and really means the aristocracy of freemen. In a democracy, the free poor, being in majority, wield the power of the states. He classified the government in the following six types on the double basis :

(1) Monarchy-based on virtue — Pure form
Tyranny — based on deceit and selfishness — Perverted Form.

(2) Aristocracy based on virtue and wealth — Pure Form.
Oligarchy — based on greed of wealth — Perverted Form.

(3) Polity — based on material virtues — Pure Form.
Democracy — based on freedom and equality — Perverted Form.

Aristotle would give ultimate sovereign power to the mass of the citizens, though the best citizens only would represent the actual governing authority and machinery. His democracy referred to the rule of the majority of citizens only, not majority of the entire population. He is, therefore, not in favour of sovereignty of the people as such.

According to Aristotle the best form of government was polity which always degenerated into democracy. Democracy was the rule of majority, not in the interest of all but in that of the poor majority.

There are some differences between Aristotle's democracy and the modern democracy. Modern democracies are larger nation-states and have a representative government. Aristotle's democracy is smallness in territory and population. Here all citizens should be capable of taking part in the work of legislation and of judging. In short to him, modern representative democracy would have meant not democracy but an oligarchy.

In this way Plato and Aristotle have expressed their views on democracy in their inimitable style.

13

The Hellenic and Universal in Plato

The political philosophy of Plato is not only an abstraction but has an intimate relation with his local Hellenic ideas and institutions. It is but natural that every philosopher formulates his theories only on the basis of the ideas of his precursors and also the material and conditions prevalent in his time. Consequently, we find in Plato both the Hellenic and also the universal elements.

Plato lived during the decline of Hellenic civilisation and culture. This period and the one preceding it left an indelible impression on his mind. The defeat of Athens by Sparta in the Peloponnesian war made the Athenians ponder over the causes of their defeat and downfall of their civilisation and culture. Socrates inspired his disciple Plato in these speculations. Plato was himself disillusioned by the democracy which put his master Socrates to death.

It is said that Plato may have laid the foundations of the Republic on abstract and dialectic but the Ideal State constructed over it had many similarities with Lycurgean institutions. Sparta played an important role in influence the thoughts of Plato. Most of the elements of Plato's Ideal State as portrayed in the Republic *viz.* common meals for rulers, community of property, military training of the youth, gymnastic exercises for women, the subordination of the individual completely to the State, the equality of sexes, State-controlled education for both men and women, the hatred of the poets and the ban or thirsty of ruling class into trade were all Spartan in origin. In Sparta, as in the Republic, the governing class confined itself only to State duties and the system ensured a rigid uniformity among citizens.

The Spartans ruthlessly sacrificed every individual or family interest to the interest of the State. In Sparta, women shared the training of men and were lent out by their husbands to procreate for the State. Sparta held gold and silver for certain classes and written laws in disfavour. The weak and deformed babies were 'exposed' on eugenic grounds. All these things of Sparta besides her successful military career and political efficiency impressed all thinking Greeks, including Plato. But Plato did not fail to see the intellectual backwardness of Sparta. So Plato did not borrow wholesale from Sparta in his Republic but tried to strike a balance between physical fitness of Sparta and intellectual keenness of Athens. But as the Republic was written when Athens was passing through the most demoralised State, the content of this book is more Spartan than Athenian. But by the time the Laws were written, Athens had recovered her lost position to a great extent, the Laws depicts, a constitution closely modelled, on the Athenian institutions, *viz.* the four-fold classification of the population according to wealth, the organisation and functions of the administrative council, recognition of law as thc golden cord of the State, the prohibition of interest on loans, the mode of choosing magistrates by election etc.

Plato did not denounce slavery, condemned trade and disallowed enslavement of the Greeks because he thought and wrote in terms of the City-States of ancient Hellas. The 'guardians' of the laws and the Nocturnal Council strongly suggest the Senate of the Areopagus. Plato fused the individualism of Athens with specialisation and absolution of Sparta. Decline of Plato's Ideal State depicts the Spartan institutions. There is also resemblance between Plato's Ideal State and Pythagorean League, an aristocracy of virtue. The literary and philosophic touch in Plato's scheme of education for the guardians was Athenian in origin from which Hellenism of Plato is clearly borne out.

The idea of training came to be approached during the time of Plato, when "a professional soldier, Iphicrats had astonished the world by showing what a body of light armed, professionally trained troops could do even against the heavy infantry of Sparta." In a negative way also the Hellas influenced Platonic thought. Often the civic unrest in Athens was primarily because of great diversities of wealth which are in consistent with good government. The factions between the rich and the poor drovc him to advocate the abolition of property. Sabine says, "The abolition of marriage was probably an implied criticism of the position of women in Athens, where her activities were summed up in keeping the house and rearing her children." In his communism of property and wives he was not only influenced by Spartan system, but also from other Hellenic practice as well as theory. Greek hunters could, by common custom take out of other people's stores. In Crete, public lands were tilled by public serfs, and the income was used for common meals and general expenses of government. Even Pythagorus remarked that friends should have all things in common. Herodotus records that the Agathyrsians held their women in common. In the Protesilaus, Euripedes advocated the community of wives.

Plato was in agreement with general Greek tradition that chief function of education was to train a citizen in the true spirit of the constitution of the State to enable him to play his due part in the State. People of his time chose education for the children as their fancies prompted or as the marked of the day provided. His educational system combined the curriculum of Athens with the administrative organisation of Sparta. That is why Sabine remarked that it was a running commentary on the existing institutions. His aversion to poetry resulted out of experience. Poets told the stories of Koruos eating his sons and daughters, talked loudly of adulteries of Aphrodite and the escapades of Leuns in the form of a swan, bull etc. Taking these into consideration Plato puts a virtual ban on poetry; with the belief that poets make States too unstable. It is evident from the above facts that there was positive Hellenic influence on Plato's thought.

Plato's writings do not have only topical interest but also contain a good deal of what is of universal value useful to mankind for all times and climes. He is one of those greatest philosophers who have contributed a great deal of original to human thought. Sabine remarks that "the Republic was the greatest of Utopias and the whole tribe of Utopian philosophers followed it." Perhaps the Ideal State portrayed in The Republic is laid in heaven and will never be realised. But we should not forget that his Ideal State was meant to be a model to be emulated. He was trying to show what in principle and in theory the State ought to be. He did not worry about its practicability. This is something which has permanent value for political science. He is the first scientific philosopher who dealt with political problems, which even now remain the same. Scientific treatment is an important legacy of his political thought.

His emphasis on justice, on the emancipation of women and their equality with men, on the rule of intellect, on functional specialisation and his principles of eugenics are of permanent importance in his political philosophy. It is a universal truth, stated by Plato, that it is only very few who have the capacity to rule while general mass is incapable of dealing with political problems. However, unpleasant it may be, but it is a fact that many modern writers and thinkers are very much disappointed with democracy. The clergy of Europe in medieval history almost resembled the philosopher guardians of Plato. They ruled for about a thousand years and their eminence rested of their mastery of religious books, and their disposition a life of meditation and simplicity. In the later half of the period they were also free from family cares. According to Will Durant the communist rulers of Russia after 1917 reminded us of the Republic. He further says, "Essentially he (Plato) is right — is he not? What this world needs is to be ruled by its wisest man? It is our business to adopt his thought to our own times and limitations."

According to Wayper, Plato portrays the unjust State in order to bring home the lesson that fall of personal conduct is the cause of lowering the moral standard of public life. Power and wealth have always corrupted men in public life. In the words of Maxey, "His mordant analysis of the fatal tendencies of free enterprise in an acquisitive society has been echoed again and again in the history of Western civilisation." Again says Maxey, "Plato's analysis of the factors in the growth and decline of States and their cycles of change reveals a genuine appreciation of the materialistic forces of historical causation. Like Marx and Lenin, he proposed to work with history and not against it."

Plato is the precursor of all great lovers of social idealism. Milton, Locke, Rousseau, Goethe etc. drank deep from his philosophy. Modern psychology is indebted to Plato's Republic in showing the importance of the unconscious and subconscious in education and significance of dreams in bringing out the lower nature of man. His ideal of an education continuing through life and extending to both sexes and the ideal of unity and correlation of knowledge are ever to be emulated by man. The modern statesman and legislator has much to learn from Plato's system of jurisprudence, his distinction between civil and criminal laws and his insistence that laws should be reformatory rather than punitive and, therefore, must have explanatory preambles.

Modern Fascism bears a close resemblance to Platonism although there are some essential points of difference. Both hate democracy, human equality and liberty and advocate dictatorship of an all-wise man and regimentation of civil life. Both believe in deification of Sate. His suggestions regarding an official survey and registry of all titles to real estates and regarding official standardisation of weights and measures are universally in practice. Plato has profoundly influenced Rousseau, Auguste Comte, Sir Thomas More and also the German and English Schools of Idealists.

Thus, Plato's thought has tremendous universal importance. Modern world has followed him a great deal in all spheres of life. He was like a philosopher of his own description; a comptroller of all being and all time. "The profound nature of his philosophy, his grasp of the fundamentals of life and his political radicalism make Plato a helpful guide for all times and places." The ideas propounded by him still loom large in the present age. That is why Barke remarks that an Englishmen feels more at house with the works of Plato in the 5th Century B.C. Rather than with the memoirs of Frederick the Great who lived in the 18th century. And Prof. Smith says, "We are the Greeks." In the words of Catlin, "The old problems (of Plato) have all come round again. The old answers are still true, eugenics, nudism, abortion, feminism communism, proletarian democracy, division of labour, class-war, scientific expertise — all the problems are here."

14

The Politicus of Plato

It is extremely fortunate that, unlike those of Aristotle, Plato's works have come down to us "whole and entire." Between the ages of 67 and 81, he wrote a number of dialogues including the Politicus and the Laws.

The Politicus or Statesman, representing a gradual transition from the idealism of the Republic to the realism of the Laws follows, to a considerable extent, the political doctrines of the Republic. According to functions, he classified the population of the state in both the treatises. The lowest class besides slaves including priests and soothsayers are engaged in industrial and practical occupation. Next is the class of those engaged in rhetoric, judging and strategy. Then comes the administrators with right knowledge of things. Finally comes statesman himself. The politicus distinguishes between statesman who trains rulers and the actual administrators.

Plato's Politicus is less ideal than the Republic. It recognises the many practical difficulties of administration in our Ideal State. Like the Republic, the Politicus stresses the necessity of education.

Plato describes the qualities and duties of a philosopher-ruler in the Politicus. Since no perfect ruler is really available, he hold that actually the only guarantee of good rule is the sovereignty of law embodied in the traditional customs of the people. This enables Plato to distinguish between good and bad forms of Government.

Plato discusses the comparative advantage of rule of law and rule of the Philosopher-ruler in the Politicus. He gives his decision in favour of the latter.

The first and foremost aim of the Politicus is to determine the characteristics and qualities, intellectual and moral, of a true ruler. He visualises government by an All-wise Monarch. His argument is based on the analogy between the physician and the statesman. Both are above rigid rules and laws.

Politicus is akin to the Republic in much of its content. In style and manner it resembles the Laws of Plato.

The Laws of Plato

Plato wrote his Laws at the ripe age of seventy. Thirty years of experience and meditation result in ripened judgement and abundance of detail. Plato is considered as a practical thinker because of his Laws. More than any of his works, the Laws reflects the political conditions prevailing in the days of Plato.

The above work of Plato, probably was finished between 360-347 B.C.

The personnel of the dialogue is very simple. There are only three characters, *viz.* an unsecured Athenian who is the principal speaker, Magillus, a Spartan and Clinias, a Cretan. The idea is to discover laws and institutions for a practicable model state.

"The manifest object of the whole work is to serve as a model for scientific students of jurisprudence and politics, who may be called upon to act as advisers to the practical statesman engaged in founding a new community or remodelling an old one."

In the Laws Plato primarily deals with politics and explains at length political institutions and physical economic and social aspects of state. He considers the community of race, language, law and religion as desirable factors for his sub-ideal state.

"The object of the greater part of the Laws is to give expert advisers from the Academy, called in to assist in undertakings of this sort, a model for their procedure."

The second state of Plato is described as half-way house between the ideal and actual state according to Barker. To Plato "Subjection is bad both for masters and for subjects."

Secondly, Plato repeatedly says in the book called the 'Laws' that his purpose is to define a second best state. This means that Plato was convinced that his Ideal State is always good but is not possible to attain it due to human nature. It was perhaps the sobriety and wisdom that came to him in his old age which made him realise this. Thirdly, the Greeks of those times believed that "to suffer injustice is better than to do injustice." Hence, in his second best state he tried to compromise the principles of his State to the popular feeling. In the 'Law' hc borrowed more from Athenian institution than from Sparta.

Comparison between the Republic and the Laws

The Republic of Plato was written in the vigour of youth with the burning zeal of a reformer and is full of hopes and inspirations. The Laws, on the other hand, reflects sobriety and maturity of judgement characterising old age and shows disillusioning experiences and knowledge of life.

The Republic has the stamp of an intellectual poem, the Laws bears that of a religious sermon.

The Republic is built on the paradoxes of the absolution of philosopher-ruler and communism of property and the Laws advocates the merits of a balanced constitution both aristocratic and democratic elements and, while renouncing communism, institutes common tables.

The Republic concentrates on the constitution of the ideal state and ignored Laws; the Laws concentrates on laws and preambles to the comparative neglect of the constitution.

Both the Republic and the Laws advocate a well regulated state-controlled system of education, that in the Laws extending not only to guardiains but to all classes. Both exclude citizens from servile occupations.

The Republic represents an abstract type-state. In the Laws, Plato tries to restore law to its proper place in the state and enters into a careful analysis of institutions and laws.

In the Republic, the city-state portrayed is, partly a Utopia and Plato himself does not believe in the practicability of it. The aim of the Republic is throughtout ethical rather than political. In the laws, Plato gives us a carefully planned and detailed scheme of a written constitution and a legal code which might contribute to the building up of a high and sound moral in the life of an actual Hellenic community in the days of Plato. He lays down some basic principles of moral and legal nature in the Laws to help constitution makers of his day. In the Laws Plato abandons the rule of the best for the rule of moderation like Aristotle.

No doubt the Laws of Plato represents a good treatise on the principles of jurisprudence. It embodies both a "theory of the constitution and a comprehensive legal code."

According to Plato the utility and stability of institutions depend upon a proper notion of individuality and its development. The foundation of constitutional and legal theory must be laid on a clear and sound doctrine of human conduct. Politics must, therefore, be a handmaid of Ethics.

According to Plato tradition and material environment are essential for society to achieve 'complete goodness'.

Plato has forceful opinion about the religion of the city-states. He says that the individual must offer his rituals and ceremonies under the auspices of the state but not according to his own free-will. He thinks that private religion withdraws men from their allegiance to the state — He is even in favour of a new creed of religion for his state and proposes to penalise by law who disbelieves in it. He proposes imprisonment and even death to athletes. There is not much difference in the scheme of education as given in the Republic and the Laws. Compulsory and similar educatin for all men and women, distrust of poets, censorship of art and literature, training in gymnastics and music — all remain unchanged. But he would now like the education to be imparted in public regulated schools by paid teachers, under the directions of a magistrate, who is the Chief of all the magistrates.

In Book III of the Laws, Plato tries to give a good constitution. The important feature of the Laws is the theory of the 'balance of constitution' by which we, moderns, set such store. To Plato, "Good government is impossible where the plenitude of sovereign power is concentrated in the hands of a single person or a single body of men." There must be a proper division of sovereign powers in a constitution which should combine the two elements of monarchy, providing personal authority and initiative and democracy, ensuring proper control of public affairs. So far as this scheme is concerned Plato may be called the father of modern constitutionalism.

Plato disagrees violently with the militaristic philosophy of life and public institutions. In his view the supreme victory is not over external enemies but over the internal enemy. It lies in "the conquest of the worst elements within the community or the personal self by the better." Peace and not war should be the end of public institution and legislation. Hence, wisdom, sobriety of soul and justice, *i.e.*, reverence for rights are the supreme virtues. Valour only takes precedence after these virtues. All these virtues, collectively make for 'complete goodness'.

BOOK I

Synopsis of the Laws. The following three propositions are dealt in detail :

(1) Peace is essential for state. It should be permanently organised for peace and not for war.

(2) The state must take 'complete goodness' for its citizens if so organised.

(3) Moral training, passion, decorum and modesty represent discipline. To obtain 'complete goodness' all these are very essential.

BOOK II

This book deals with the cultivation of a child's moral sense through its taste and imagination, *i.e.*, by "learning to feel pleasure and pain about the right things." There should be the cultivation of taste and character through taste.

The aim of education should be to minimise divergence between taste and judgement.

Plato, then, dilates on music and the cultivation of the musical sense.

BOOK III

This book deals with one of the main problems of a political philosopher. Further Plato explains what "a city" is and how it arises. He applies the genetic method. He also tries to trace the origin of law and of constitutional order as also their functions and the conditions necessary for them. This is philosophy of History in its first inception.

"Balance in the Constitution" is a necessary one for the permanent well-being of every state. It is a division of the sovereign power between several organs of government. Concentration of sovereign power in one hand is fatal and mortal. Monarchy and Democracy are the two indispensible elements of constitution. According to Plato in the political communities reason must rule through law.

BOOK IV

The topography on the political machinery of the state is beautifully discussed in this book. Legal and constitutional institutions, agricultural economy and the economic resources are clearly dealt in this book. Plato is against a large trade which would necessitate a strong navy and would lead to a policy and spirit of aggressive imperialism. National greatness lies not in wealth and dominion, but in intellect and character. Plato's views against cosmopolitanism is very impressive and interesting. Plato analyses the possibility of institutions which will 'promote complete goodness.'

Laws, according to Plato, should be directive no less than punitive or retributive.

Every man must follow good to lead the life of right 'measure'.

A man must first care for virtue and wisdom, than health and lastly wealth.

It is the duty of the citizens to help the authorities in the chastisement of crime, though in a merciful and not vindictive spirit.

BOOK V

This book deals with the problem of actual social and political construction which will provide a systematic body of legislation and an executive of magistrates and official boards to put this legislation into effect. The executive must be composed of men of tasted superiority of understanding and strength of character.

Plato fixes the number of citizens at 5040. The society should not be organised on 'communistic' lines. Economic inequalities must be prevented as far as possible. He also suggest the division of society into four property classes. Certain important executive posts should be reserved for members of wealthy classes. Plato divides the population of the city-state into twelve tribes and the capital into twelve corresponding districts for administrative convenience.

BOOK VI

Magistracies and administrative boards are dealt in this book as mentioned below :

The "Curators of Law" the most important magistracies are mentioned in this book. It consists of 37 members of proved intelligence and character, aged between 50 and 70. Their duty is to watch the administration of law in general, keep registers of properties, penalise those who conceal their incomes and be judges in trials of grave offences.

The "Executive Council" is to be the representative chamber of 36 members. One-twelfth of the whole body will form the monthly action committee.

There will be the Urban Commissioners and Rural Commissioners.

The Minister of Education must be elected out of the Curators of Law and must be over 50 in age with his own children.

According to Plato a good social order depends on a wholesome family life. Regulation of marriages, proper selection of mates and prohibition of dowries are mentioned in this book. He advocates an institution of a baord of ladies to supervise the conduct of married couples for the first ten years from the point of view of morality and eugenics. The state must keep a record of all births and deaths. No man under 30 and woman under 40 should hold office.

BOOK VII

In this book, Plato discusses about education. It must be under public control from the beginning.

According to Plato, children must begin to receive judicious correction at the age of three. Their games must be superintended by ladies up to the age of six. At the age of six regular lessons may begin. The girls must be segregated from boys. The girls must learn riding and the use of weapons. They must specialise in dancing and wrestling. They must learn music which leads to the training of taste and intelligence.

According to Plato a good system of education will require schools with proper buildings, adequate grounds and expert teachers, such schools must be state-controlled and state-aided. For both sexes attendance must be compulsory.

Arithemetic, Astronomy and Music are taught upto the age of 16. Added to this reading and writing are also taught to them during this period. After these elementary studies, there should be a study of higher Arithmetic, Geometry and Astronomy.

BOOK VIII

In this book, Plato deals about the religious sanction of the society, its ritual of worship and the right social tradition. Moreover, it deals with torts and agrarian disorders. All industry must be in the hands of aliens.

BOOK IX

Plato, in this book, deals with criminal jurisprudence. The distinction between criminal law and civil law of torts is clearly pictured by Plato. It obviously shows his originality.

Moreover, this book deals with all branches of violation of public and private rights.

BOOK X

The foundation of all subsequent 'natural' theology is found in this book. It tries to "demonstrate God's existence and moral government of the world from the known facts of the visible order." It makes the first known suggestion for the erection of an Inquisition — *Atheism, deism* and *the doctrine that a sinner can escape divine judgement by prayers and sacrifices*, were posionous to the moral life of the society according to Plato. Magistrates must deal with cases of impiety.

BOOK XI

This book deals with out and out a series of enactments against less serius offences.

BOOK XII

Plato deals with public law in this book. It indicates the misconduct of ambsssadors and embezzlement of public funds. A board of twelve must supervise and scrutinize the work of magistrates, relating to the audit of public funds.

Plato allows foreign travel under license. The 'Nocturnal Council' — the Board of Twelve is invested with constant and supreme supervision and maintenance of national life, based on one single aim, *i.e.*, 'complete goodness'. "It is evident that this Nocturnal Council stands in the place of the philosopher-king of the Republic and that its inclusion in the Laws is a flagrant violation of loyalty to the Second Best State." In short the members of this body must be animated with godliness resting on knowledge.

15

The Theory of the State in the Laws

In his Republic, Plato had portrayed the Ideal State in a graphic manner. After that he wrote the Laws, his views had undergone some change. The re-emergence of law in his later writings is a matter of great importance in the estimate of his political philosophy. This implies drastic changes in all the underlying principles of government. In his Ideal State the philosopher-ruler was the "guardian of the Republic" unfettered by law; in the "second best" state the ruler is the "guardian of the law," the servant and slave of law.

According to Plato the legislator, while framing Laws, must keep certain basic principles in view. "Self-control" means a free concord of appetite with reason. It is clear, therefore, that if the legislator so frames, and adjusts his laws to produce in a state the complete virtue of self-control, he will attain three ends in one, *i.e.*, his city-state will be free, will be united and will be possessed of understanding. Virtue is identified with justice. It is the virtue of self-control which becomes the mainspring of the Laws.

Plato says that the rulers of the Laws have political, economic and social rights. The same applied to the ruled. The rulers have private property and family. Communism of property and family are now abandoned though common tables for men and women are still retained. The ruled have a voice and a vote in the election of their rulers. Such a state based on self-control, will have the unity of sympathy born of harmonious cooperation.

Plato is against a war state. Each state should look to an inward war to bring about final peace and lasting reconciliation through the harmony which comes of moderation and self-control.

The Nature of Law in the State

The foremost aim of law is to express the ideals of every state. Plato explains the following with regard to nature of law :

1. Necessity of Law,
2. Origin of Law,
3. Extent of Law and
4. Sovereignty of Law.

1. Necessity of Law. 'Law is civilisation' is found in the passage of the Book IX of Plato. The law is necessary because (i) our individual minds are not competant to recognise what is the best in social life; (ii) our individual wills are not always able to or willing to pursue the best and (iii) we need law to precipitate and crystallise the good for us.

2. Origin of Law. According to Plato the conflict of the customs of different families in early societies involved the need of a legislator for the purpose of comparing the different customs and selecting the best for adoption. Plato held that the effects of war, influence of economic conditions, pestilence, famine are our legislators.

3. Extent of Law. Law is the expression of mind or reason and is of universal import. It extends over the whole life since it is one with reason.

4. Sovereignty of Law. Law must be supreme in a law-state. Law must function in the interest of all in the state. Government must be controlled in the interest of all.

Plato had a firm belief in the sovereignty of law. At the same time he had the same belief in the rigidity of law. He thinks of a fundamental law to which the actions of the rulers and the ruled must conform.

Laws may be rigidly applied, it should be accompanied by prefaces and preambles, which enunciate the principles on which laws are based and which show to people that laws are based on principles popularly believed and acceptable. Law is the expression of sovereign reason and may take the form of a sovereign command; but they are also the vehicle of the virtue of self-control, which represents a harmony between reason and appetite — the two basic virtues and elements of society. The preambles must achieve this harmony by adding persuasion to command.

The two elements of persuasion and command will find their political parallel in a mixed constitution on which democratic and monarchical elements are blended.

Laws with their preambles give us not a rule of bare law, but a rule of the philosophic law.

Plato's law regulates the whole of our moral life. It should be enforced, not only by punishment and by the state but also by education and by appeal to mind.

On the whole law trains the young to right reason and in perfect citizenship.

Economic structure of the State in the Laws

As regards property, an individual is given right to private property but under strict state supervision. Plato fixed the number of citizens to 5040. Wealth is to come from land. The land is to be equally divided among citizens. It will be inherited but not divided or alienated. The produce of the land is to be consumed in common at a public mass. The cultivation of land is to be done by slaves or serfs. Personal property is permitted but its amount is limited *i.e.*, Plato would prohibit to any citizen a personal property exceeding four times of the lot of land. The purpose is to exclude large differences between the rich and the poor. Besides, Plato does not permit his citizens to engage themselves in business, trade or industry, which he reserves for resident aliens, who are freemen but not citizens. Moreover, he prohibits the taking of interest for loans and the possession of gold and silver. Thus, instead of a complete abnegation of property and advocated in the Republic Plato gives a new and modified communism with division of land accompanied by safeguards against concentration of wealth. Here he gives a new division of labour. Agriculture is the function of slaves, trade and industry that of resident aliens and political functions are the privilege of the citizens.

Social structure of the State in the Laws

In the Laws, Plato insists on the right and the duty of women to take their place by the side of men in the general life of the state. He insists also that women should have the same education as men and be free to follow the same pursuits. He abandons the community of wives and children. He still holds that women should be drawn into public life by a system of common tables and that marriage should be controlled in the public interest. Plato holds the views that women must be trained in gymnastics and must share in the contest of boys. They might share in tournaments, fight on horseback and fight by the side of men in case of war. Plato does not suggest that women should hold any office or vote in the assembly. Women are connected with the institution of marriage as supervisors.

According to Plato there is no women guardians as in the Republic.

Permanent monogamous unions, with an intolerable amount of public supervision, are accepted as the lawful form of marriage. Women are to give birth to children only between the age of twenty and forty. Every couple is required to produce a certificate of good health before mating. In the Laws, Plato not only permits marriage, but would penalise bachelors over 35 years of age.

The System of Government in the Laws

In his book the Laws Plato has asserted the fundamental principle of Sovereignty of Laws. He has expressed the view that in the second best state law is sovereign and supreme and the Government with all its organs should be subordinate to it. No body of magistrates, no council or senate or no assembly, however broad will be other than subordinate to the law. But Plato does not maintain this thesis in the Twelfth Book. The most important reason for the absence of any sovereign body in the government is that the institution of the sub-ideal state must be mixed type. It should be a reconciliation of monarchy with democracy, the principle of knowledge with the principle of liberty. A mixed constitution can hardly contain a single sovereign authority.

In this context, Prof. Barker says, "It is impossible to say of the constitution of Sparta, whether it is a monarchy or an aristocracy, a tyranny or democracy, it must be equally impossible to say of the state, which Plato builds in the Laws that it is ruled by any one sovereign authority."

In the Platonic state of laws, the electoral authority is a popular assembly, which elects the council and the various executive magistrates. This popular assembly is the whole body of 5000 citizens, arranged in four classes on the basis of property qualification, according to the differences in the amount of the property possessed by them. It is a compulsion for the first two classes to attend the meetings, but for the 3rd and 4th class attendance is optional. Besides this, no citizen of any class may attend these meetings unless he bears arms and has gone through military service.

The functions of the assembly are to elect the guardians of the law and the council. It also elects number of local officials and generals of the army. The 37 guardians of the law are to be elected by a triple ballot. In the first ballot 300 are elected; in the second ballot 200 are eliminated and only 100 are elected. In the third and final ballot 37 are elected from the hundred candidates who remain.

The election of the council is much more elaborate than that of the assembly and the election of 37 guardians. The council is to consist of 350 members. They are elected annually. Ninety members are elected from each of the four classes. Different ways are followed in the selection of the above ninety members. The whole system is a carefully calculated combination of universal suffrage with class-suffrage as well as a combination of the Greek aristocratic method of election by voting with democratic method of ballot. "Plato defends the system as a mean between the monarchical principle of wisdom and the democratic principle of liberty."

The popular assembly has the following functions :

(1) It elects the council.

(2) It elects the local officials of the city and market.

(3) It elects the generals of the army.

(4) It has cognizance of public suits against those who have injured the state.

(5) Its consent is necessary if any law has to be changed.

(6) It has the power of extending the stay of resident aliens beyond the appointed period of 20 years.

The popular assembly plays a double part as an electorate and as a judicature but it has no deliberative functions.

Plato's council is to be divided into 12 divisions, each division acting for a month as the main organ of government and the presiding body in the state. Each division in its turn, is to act in co-operation with the executive magistrates, *i.e.*, Guardians of laws (37 in number) elected by the popular assembly for a term of 20 years. Their age must be between 50 and 70.

Each division, during its tenure of office, in audience, foreigners and citizens and dissolve the meeting of the assembly, whether it be for election, for justice or for a change in the laws.

As regards judicial institutions of the State, Plato distinguishes between private and public suits. For private suits, there are to be three graders of courts :

(1) Voluntary court,
(2) Tribal court and
(3) Court of select judge.

(1) **Voluntary Courts.** This Court is composed of neighbours and friends who know the issue best. According to Plato this court has 'Greater competence'.

(2) **Tribal Court.** The judges of this court are to be chosen by lot. In such court, the principle of a popular judicature is recognized. Prof. Barker says "that principle is one on which Plato lays emphasis; all should have a share in jurisdiction for the man who does not share in the power of sitting with others in justice and think himself utterly without any part in the state."

(3) **The court of select judges.** The judges are annually chosen by all the magistrates of the state in conjuction. The sittings of these courts shall be public and decisions delivered in open court.

Local Government

The form of Local-government described by Plato is slight. A state of 5040 persons can need little beyond its Central Government. In the central city there are :

(a) City inspectors, and
(b) Inspectors of the market square.

The city inspectors are concerned with the care of the city, its buildings, its roads, water supply, while the market inspectors superintend the market square and its buildings and business. Both type of inspectors, however, have a petty jurisdiction.

Prof. Barker has given his analysis on the 'System of Government in the Laws' in an exemplary manner.

The Theory of Law in the Laws

Plato's Laws, as the first attempt made in Greece to frame a legal code is not merely based on the Laws of a single state but embraces Greek law in general and is not a mere tabulation but a scientific study based on the first principles of social conduct. It is a serious contribution to jurisprudence presented by legal sense and going into legal detail. Plato gives legal procedure, discusses the law of contract of succession and of property in general.

Plato's law is subject to modern criticism that it is morality and even theology as well as law. There is clear cut distinction between legality and morality or religion. The legal code contains much of moral philosophy or even moral theology.

In the 9th Book of the Laws Plato has given a beautiful account about crime and its punishment. A true state will take a higher view of its own functions and of the rights of the criminal. Laws should be loving and wise parents should train as well as punish. Administration of law is education; punishment is reformation and its object is to act on the mind so as to produce a conversion of character. Crime is the result of moral disease and should be cured as such.

The criminal is forced to be free of his moral disease. Plato has got a reformatory view of punishment which is awarded not to inflict harm to the criminal but to make him better. Plato at once believes in the wickedness of the crime and real goodness of man's mind. He emphasizes the responsibility of society for corruption which leads to crime. The society must remove this corruption.

Though punishment is held to be reformatory and not retributive, actual punishments recommended by Plato are rather severe and rigorous. Treason, faction, sacrilege, forms of religious unbelief, advocacy of better appearing worse, theft of public property, misconduct of magistrates, receiving of exiles and bribe taking and contempt of decisions of court of law are chief crimes found in the list deserving capital punishment.

Moreover, Plato advocates religious persecution of (1) honest disbelievers, who are otherwise good men and citizens to be imprisoned for 5 years in the House of Reformation. If after release they are again convicted of disbelief, they are to be put to death. (2) Dishonest disbelievers (against the religion of the state) are to be imprisoned for life. (3) Those practising "private religions" are also to be persecuted. It is on the whole intended to promote the unity of the state.

The Theory of Education in the Laws

According to Plato the law is fixed and the substance and curriculum of education must be equally fixed.

Plato assigns higher place to education. Education is to be under the supervision of the Minister of Education. He is to be the Prime Minister in the state. He is to be chosen from amongst the Guardians of the Laws by an electoral body of all the magistrates. He must be a man of 50 years of age, married and father of children.

The system of education in the state must be under state regulation and control.

The function of the Minister of Education is to direct administration and education in gymnasia and schools, to regulate attendance, and to supervise buildings. Education judges *i.e.*, examiners and inspectors who control competitive tests and awards prizes, both in gymnastics and in music are under his direct control. He also advocates a single school system in which teachers can teach all subjects instead of parents sending their children to different teachers for different subjects. He further advocates a system of universal compulsory education. He does not advocate co-education. But he advocates the training of both sexes on parallel lines in gymnastics and music.

According to Plato the scheme of primary education begins with the cradle. It is the duty of the Nurses to train the babies from the age of three in shouting and jumping. After three, the children to be taken by the Nurses to the village temples to play under supervision. At the age of six, the sexes are separated; now their studies begin in the shape of physical drill. Riding, archery and the use of sling are taught to both sexes.

The secondary education begins at the age of 10. There needs to be a tutor for him. The boy must study literature, *i.e.*, learn to read and write, acquire some knowledge of lyre, elements of arithmetic and geometry and astronomy.

From above it is obvious that the Secondary Education embraces three subjects, *i.e.*, literature, music and elementary mathematics. The study of literature is to last from 10 to 13, of music from 13 to 16, Arithmetic comes in between.

Since gymnastic is an essential part of education, it is clear that military training is an essential part of Plato's educational system.

At the age of 16, education would seem to have been completed. The Laws stop short at primary and secondary education.

Estimate

The Laws of Plato tremendously influenced later thought from Aristotle onwards. Ethics of Aristotle echoes the Laws. No wonder the political and educational principles laid down in Aristotle's Politics are also modelled on the Laws. The 'Ideal State' of Aristotle is the 'city' of the Laws minus the Nocturnal Council.

In spite of his criticism of the Laws, Aristotle has borrowed a good deal from the last great classic of Plato. In his Politics Aristotle adopts Plato's conception of the sovereignty of law and 'guardians of the law and its servants. The development of the state from the family and the partriarchal character of the early states are taken from the Book III of the Laws. Aristotle follows the same idea of Plato in respect of the theory of mixed constitution. Aristotle views about the importance of agriculture and about retail trade and usury are identical with those of Plato in the Laws. Plato defends compulsory education for children. Similarly Aristotle argues for common public education for them.

The influence of Plato on the writers of later period cannot be misused or underestimated. The writer of the Hellenic and Greco-Roman period show familiarity with the Laws. The Christian Fathers quote its moral and religious sanctions. Direct contact with the Laws came with the Renaissance. The Seventeenth century Anglicanism borrowed from the Laws which also made a special appeal to Ruskin. Sir Thomas Moore's Utopia is based on the Laws as well as on the Republic of Plato.

In modern times, many of the constitutional, legal and educational innovations are based on the Laws, to which also is traceable the modern Inquisition.

The secondary schools and Academies of the Hellenic cities and Greco-Roman period owe their inspiration to the Laws.

Plato's Academy may be said to be the first 'incorporated University'.

Plato's Laws from the point of view of jurisprudence, has influenced the development of Roman Law, which incorporates 'jus gentium', and 'jus gentium' was substantially Greek law which must have borrowed considerably from the Platonic jurisprudance. It is the basis of the systems of jurisprudence of many European and American nations.

Plato's chief contributions of the Laws are considered as everlasting features. A clear enunciation of the principles of constitutional or divided sovereignty and the training and education of infants, children and young persons are really worthy features. Added to this the definite creation of 'natural theology' and the distinction between criminal jurisprudence and the law of civil torts are monumental contributions of Plato. Recognition of the necessity of an official survey and registration of all titles to real estates, official standardization of weights and measures, the gradations of the prisons of the state and regulations regarding judicial proceedings are other contributions of the Laws.

Thus, the Laws of Plato has profoundly influenced later thought from Aristotle onwards.

16

Plato As A Fascist

It is generally noticed that great thinkers have always aroused controversial comments from later critics. They evoke contradictory interpretation by their protagonists and denunciators. Among such philosophers we can name Rousseau, Hobbes, Hegel, Marx besides Plato. Thus, some scholars have dubbed Plato as the first fascist. Prominent among them are Dr. Popper and Bertrand Russel. Neitzsche accused both Socrates and Plato of being the fathers of the Decadence in Hellenic culture. Bertrand Russell says that "Plato's Republic should have been admired, on its political side, by decent people, is perhaps the most astonishing example of literary snobbery in all history." On the other hand, he is known as Divine Plato and Catlin says, "The old man is dead twentytwo centuries ago, but human nature does not die and precisely his love of abstract truth about that nature have saved him from obscurity." The old problems have all come round again — eugenics, communism, democracy, class-war and what not.

Firstly, the antagonism of Plato to democracy is much taken to task in the writings of these critics. Plato wanted all the books of Democritics, a great champion of democracy, to be burnt. His main charge against democracy is that it is too tolerant; allows even the asses to walk on the footpath; as not standards of value, etc. According to him, democracy denounces discipline and order. It was this democracy that to had put death, his master, Socrates. Plato repudiates human equality and distinguishes between a citizen and a slave and citizen and citizen *i.e.* thinkers and non-thinkers. Fascism also believes that only a few persons have got the capacity to lead and guide the nation. According to Fascists, democracy is a farce. Democracy means inefficiency and chaos, rule of the poor and fools. Plato regards democracy, like Fascists as the worst of Governments.

It was this poor opinion about democracy that made him to richly borrow from the example of Sparta. That is why Bertrand Russell says Pelopponesion War concentrated the struggle that was taking place throughout the Hellenic world between Democracy and Oligarchy, and the friends and family of Plato supported the cause of Sparta which stood Oligarchy. After the defeat of democratic Athens, Plato sat to work to sing the praises of the victorious by constructing an Utopia of which the main features were suggested by the contribution of Sparta. There is no one denying the fact that Plato had a very low opinion of democracy, but it should be remembered that it was born out of his experience but not due to any prejudice or aristocratic contempt.

Second argument of the critics is that Plato wánts the State to be governed by a small Oligarchy, "Who are to practise trickery and lying-trickery in manipulating the drawing of lots for eugenic purposes and elaborate lying to persuade the population that there are biological differences between the upper and lower classes." This is a curious parallel to the Fascist Philosophy. Plato's faith in the rule of intellect led him to consider the minority rule of the guardians to be the best practical form of Government. Fascism also stands for the rule of Fascist intellect and the minority rule of the Fascist Party. Dictatorship of the leader of the Fascist Party is equivalent to that of the philosopher-king. Both of them are exalted in their respective theories.

However, this argument too can be exonerated on the ground that the liberal interpretation of Plato is correct in the past, in the present and in the future also. As Bryce said, "It is always an elite that governs whether the government is a monarchy, aristocracy, oligarchy or democracy." According to Collingwood, Plato's guardians were only path finders. They were not really rulers, but mentors, guides and philosophers. This is true of the three tenses — past, present and future. In the ancient times, in Egypt and India, it was the priestly class that guided the destinies of their countries. In the medieval ages, it was the Clergy that dominated European history. In the Industrial Era, for some time, the Aristocratic class and for some time, the Bourgeois class, piloted the ship of the State. In the modern Communist State, the Communist Party alone plays the dictating rule as the vanguard of the working classes. In a democracy, it is the dimogogues that fool the majority. In this manner, a few individuals guiding the destiny of the nation is axiomatic. What all Plato desired is that this oligarchy should be trained as devotees of service. This argument takes the wind out of the sails of the critics.

Thirdly, Plato's educational scheme goes to prove him as a fascist. The main principle of his rigid scheme of education, to which everything is subordinated, is to produce courage in battle according to critics. They say, Plato wants to create a courageous State. He has made military training compulsory. This makes one believe that he was preparing the country for war-like Fascists to whom, in war lies the glory of the nation. Both advocate rigid state-controlled education. Unfortunately, we forget the fact that his main objective of the state-sponsored education is to incline the philosopher-rulers with a sense of service and devotion. They are not expected to play the same role as the Fascist leaders, who made their way up by their gift of the gab and playing on the despondency of the people. The Fascist leaders were only men of the gutter whereas the Philosopher-rulers are well-trained, educated and disciplined people. Moreover, Plato was definitely against a policy of aggressive warfare and imperialism as against imperialist ideology of Fascists.

The fourth argument is that in his education scheme, "There is to be a rigid censorship of the stories told by mothers and nurses to young children; there is to be no reading to Homer; the drama is to be forbidden as it contains villains and women; music is to be only of certain kinds, which, in modern times, would be the National Anthem." Catlin says, "Literature may also poison the climate of the good State. There will certainly no free press. On the contrary, literature will be censored." To Plato, music and poetry, if harmful to the interests of the State, should be strictly censored by the State. It means the interest of the State are supreme to everything else. This line of attack is indeed strong. All the same, it is to be remembered that Plato prohibits all these things mainly due to the ruthlessness of logic. In order that his Ideal State may be realised, he mercilessly brushed aside all that stood in the way. The same is the case with any phil sopher *par excellence*. So these drawbacks of Plato can be pardoned on this score. The Fascists believed in the regimentation of thought with the sole objective of obedience and even servitude. In the case of Plato the objective of education is to instil an ascetic spirit into philosopher guardians and it is restricted only to them.

Critics opine that both Platonism and Fascism advocate absorption of the individual by the State. According to Socrates, to obey the State whether it is just or unjust, is the duty of an individual. Plato also believed in the fascist concept of utter subordination to the State. To him the State is a magnified individual and it represents the highest manifestation of human virtue. An individual has no separate entity other than the State. There was no question of man of the State. This is exactly the deification of State by the Fascists, who believed that duty, discipline and sacrifice must bind the individual to the State. "Liberty is not a right, but a duty." To Fascists, the individual has no right except a duty — to obey the dictates of the leader.

Despite this identity of views, Plato, unlike Fascists, cannot be wholly accused of having sacrificed the individual altogether at the altar of the State. It is only the microscopic minority of the guardians whom he makes merge themselves in the State and not the masses and the producing classes. In fact, it is for the good of the mass that he would sacrifice the guardians who stand for the State. He thus conceives of the good of the subjects to be identical with the good of the State. He demands the sacrifice of the ruler and not of the subjects.

In other words, the critics argue that whether people are happy in this community does not matter, for excellence resides in the whole and not in parts. In Fascist thought, the deification of the National Personality is an extension of this principle. But it is to be stated, Plato never dreamt even that his philosopher guardians are to trample on the people. The silence of Plato, whether his Ideal State contributes for the happiness of the people, is not due to the reason that he took it for granted that it will result in happiness. His silence only indicates that he might have expected the happiness of the people as the inevitable end of his Ideal State.

Both Plato and Fascists stand for supremacy of law and order. To Plato, it is difficult to have a real philosopher to rule the State in an ideal way, laws are necessary. Fascism is also more for law than for liberty. First essential of the State is its stability. To Plato, City-State is supreme reality and to Fascists the Nation-State is supreme reality. Although both exalt their respective States, but the City-State does not want to expand but to remain as small as possible. On the other hand, the Fascist nation seeks expansion which means imperialism. Plato subordinates politics to ethics; he rather ethicised politics, but Fascism subordinates ethics to politics, as everything is to be under the State. Plato advocates communism of property and women, but Fascism represents, in Hegelian terms, the dialectic antithesis of communism. Plato is idealist and Fascists are realists, who think after they act.

According to Neitzsche, the rule of the strong has been destroyed by Plato's belief in the rule of the just. He says that the hallmark of Plato's State is not courage, but intellectualism and belief in other worldliness, which has sounded the deathnell of civilisation, according to him. So, there are many points in Plato's philosophy which when taken out of their proper context, would indicate that he is an authoritarian or Fascist to the core, or a communist or any such odious champion, but a clinical view always refutes his perverse approach.

17

Plato as Inductive and Deductive Philosopher

To observe facts and then to come to universal truth is called the inductive method. On the other hand, to take one universal truth and then to come to the conclusions is called the deductive method. Plato used deductive method in his writings, but at the same time, observed inductive method also. Deductive method had a firm hold on Plato, but he tried to give a colouring or embellishments to his deductive method by the help of inductive facts. He was purely deductive in his arguments but used inductive facts only when he accepted the human nature to be weak and frail. We cannot, however, say that inductive method was the basis of his philosophy.

Plato, in his exposition of philosophy, believed faithfully in the Socratic doctrine that virtue is knowledge. Socrates in his times, threw the challenge that if there is any valuable thinking, it must be defined. So, naturally, Plato his disciple, said that real virtue was only the ultimate idea of "Good." Virtue is knowledge and it can be acquired by the philosopher guardians of the ideal State. When this all-wise philosopher is the ruler, then will come into existence his Ideal State.

After having stated what is true virtue and who is the person that can attain, he came down to earthly realities. That is to say, he did not merely live in his fancy world of abstract thinking. He said that human nature is composed of the three psychological characteristics called reason, spirit and appetite. After taking this thing granted, he states that in the philosopher-rulers or kings, reasons will dominate, in the military guardians the spirit will dominate, and in the workers and artisans, appetite will dominate.

Then, Plato argues that as men are endowed with different capacities, they must try to develop that quality alone. That is to say that each person, according to his ability, must specialise in his own field. This is called the functional specialisation.

The next question was how to develop this ability. In order to make them perfect in their own respective fields, he advocated a system of State education. With the help of education, the individual will be able to perceive the 'Idea of Good.' It will result in the beautification of soul which means the inward eye of the individual will totally perceive the innerly light.

While discussing about the philosopher-rulers, he finds that often the rulers in the actual State were distracted by two institutions called family and property. Hence, he pleaded to distroy both of them. Thus, it is clear from the step of definition of what is real virtue, he derives all these important conclusions.

Inductive

Plato has also used inductive method to modify his deductive conclusions. He borrowed certain things from the ancient thought. The first thing he borrowed from Sparta was discipline. In Sparta men used to dine at common table and they were most disciplined people. Plato tried to develop a sense of discipline among the Athenians also, as stated in his Ideal State. Dunning says, "Plato Spartanised his Athenians."

When he thought that his Ideal State was too good to be attained owing to the weakness and frailty of human nature, he made law to be sovereign in his second best State. In the Republic Plato excludes law altogether, but when he was faced with realities, he gave law a significant place (in the 'Laws' and the 'Statesman'). In the words of Ferguson, "Whoever pays the obedience of the child and courts deals like Socrates is a true Greek." This shows the significance of law in those times.

His scheme of education was a happy blend of the educational systems in Sparta and Athens. He combined the curriculum of Athens with organisation of Sparta. The Spartan education at that time was highly disciplined. What all he did was, he transformed the existing system of education to fit into his realisation of the Ideal State. He has adopted the same curriculum found in those times in his Ideal State. He suggested that the education should be imparted by the State as was done in Sparta. Education leads to the realisation of the 'Good'. He shaped the existing education to his own purpose.

Plato's idealism and communism were not entirely unrelated to Hellenic life of his day. He had before him the actual example of Sparta where boys were taken from the parents at the age of 7, and brought up and educated by the State. The weak and deformed babies were 'exposed' to death. Wives were lent to procreate for State purposes. In Sparta, people, especially the ruling class, used to take their meals on one table and discuss their problems. The system of dining together at one place was one minor detail of communism that was borrowed by Plato from Sparta. In Crete there was public tilling of public estates.

The classification of States as detailed by Plato in his writings was based on the different degenerated State in Hellenic world. The 'guardians' of the Laws and the Nocturual Council strongly suggest the Senate of the Acropagus. This constitution of his second best State contains many Athenian institutions such as the four-fold classification of the population according to wealth, the organisation and functions of the administrative council, the prohibition of interest on loans, the mode of election of magistrates by election and lot. Plato thought and wrote in terms of the city-states of ancient Hellas, Plato fused the individualism of Athens with specialisation and absolutism of Sparta. The censorship of art and literature and hatred of poets were borrowed from Sparta. There is also resemblance between Plato's Ideal State and the Pythagorean League, an aristocracy of virtue.

In this manner, Plato took all these facts from the actual examples before his eyes. This was inductive method in his philosophy. To conclude, Plato used the deductive method in his writings but he took the help of inductive facts to bring certain modifications to suit his philosophy.

18

The Influence of Socrates on Plato

Plato was the greatest disciple of Socrates. He was deeply influenced among others by Socrates. This influence was so great that it is difficult to disengage what is Socratic from what is genuinely Platonic in the writings of Plato. He came under the influence of Socrates at the age of twenty and remained his pupil, nay his disciple, for eight years till his death. The execution of Socrates shocked him profoundly. It produced in his repulsion towards the political career for which he was brought up and trained because of his noble birth. He came to realise that a saint like Socrates was a misfit in the Athens of those days. He concluded from this misfortune "that the philosopher and the politician not only lacked unity of purpose in the world, but were even antagonistic."

Plato came to be convinced of the fact that "it was a Socrates that politics needed most." He made up his mind to bridge the gulf between things as they are and as they should be. He, therefore, wanted to establish that the good State is the just State in which wisdom ruled. In short, it became his mission in life to justify Socrates. He, therefore, set to himself the task of constructing an Ideal State in which a Socrates, *e.g.* a philosopher-king, would be the guiding influence. This is what he does in his masterpiece, the Republic.

In his works, Plato followed the dialectic method in the foot-steps of his illustrious master. In his dialogues he makes Socrates as the principal speaker, through whose mouth he expounds his own philosophy. Like his master, he aimed at awakening thought in his readers and not at instilling knowledge into them. His dialogues expose falsehood and after eliminating faults in various things reach the final truth. His method of analogies is also drawn from Socrates.

It was the mission of Socrates to convince men of their ignorance and to reform the moral nature of man. Like his master, Plato also had an instinctive inclination for practical reform of men and affairs. He was friend and advisor of King Dionysius of Syracuse, whom he tried his best to reform. Plato agreed with Socrates in identifying virtue with knowledge.

Virtue was knowledge, held Socrates, and single virtues were varieties of knowledge. Knowledge was the source of virtues like courage, temperance and justice. Knowledge disciplined and moulded the will and emotions. Another Socratic doctrine adopted by Plato is the doctrine of the ideal being the real. This doctrine, in the words of Coker, is :

> "Reality inheres only in the ideas of things — that is, in the perfect, permanent, immunable, self-existent entities which underlie the changing and imperfect object of perception; the latter are merely the superficial appearance of things. Plato interpreted and developed his theory and its ethical application in the identification of virtue with knowledge of absolute reality."

To Plato, the world of reality lay embedded in and behind the world of perception. What was real not a particular concrete table but the table, *e.g.*, the abstract idea embodied in the concrete table. Socratic knowledge was intimately related with character. "Know thyself" was his motto. To him, knowledge was not something grasped by the intellect alone. It was something with which the whole mind or soul was identified; it was knowledge touched with emotion; it was realisation. The political implication of Socratic doctrine of the identity of virtue with knowledge, drawn by Socrates and also Plato led them to emphasise the need of special knowledge on the part of the rulers.

Socrates rejected the belief that there is a special art of human conduct requiring a special type of goodness. On the contrary he held that it was an architectonic art and the goodness — requisite for it was a general goodness. It was a goodness of the whole soul and issued in a harmony of all its activities. It made him criticise democracy which assumed that any man can fill any office. He objected to the use of lot for selection of office bearers because it treated as equal those who had knowledge and those who lacked it totally. According to Socrates, only wise should rule and guide the State. This notion of Socrates led Plato to develop his theory of philosopher-king who rules by means of his trained intelligence, untrammelled by laws.

Plato, not only disliked democracy because of the fact that the wisest few should rule the State, but also he hated democracy which had condemned to death 'the wisest, justest and best of all the men he had ever known,' and assigned a very low place to it in his classification of States. Not only Socrate's whole life but his death also was marked by a steady discharge of his civic duty. His friends and advisers urged him to escape from prison, but he refused to disobey law. According to him, while a citizen must follow his own conscience, it was his duty to bow to the laws of the State and its judicial decisions, whether just or unjust. 'Socrates, like Hobbes, asserted the uncompromising authority and irresponsibility of the ruling power.' Plato, likewise, makes his State absolute and wants the individual to obey unquestioningly. Plato, along with Socrates, believed that man was essentially social and the State performed a necessary and useful function.

Following Socrates, Plato presupposes certain moral forms of ideas as the Good, the Just, the Beautiful, the Pious, without which we cannot characterise individual cases as being good, just, beautiful or pious. There is a deep grief between the world of Ideas. It is the business of man, as standing between these two worlds, to mediate between these and to evolve pure knowledge. The Platonic picture of the world is an ascent from becoming to being, *i.e.,* to the being of Ideas. Only by reference to the Ideas can the visible world be understood. Plato believed that man, by well directed reasoning, could arrive at probable truths, *i.e.,* positive knowledge. This scientific knowledge be applied to hit politics, which included our modern politics, ethics, metaphysics, sociology, religion etc. The chief aim of Plato was to promote justice and virtue. He tried to conjure up a vision of an ideal State where justice and virtue reign supreme.

19

Plato on Foreign Relations

Plato in his Republic tries to give a clear picture of foreign relations of his Ideal State. He turns to the question of foreign relations of his Ideal State after completing the structure of his Ideal State and after explaining and justifying its intricasies in an exemplary manner.

"He advocates", Writes Barker, "a foreign policy of alliance, or at any rate amity, among the states of Greece in opposition to Barbarions. The part of the Republic in which this argument is developed is perhaps the most definitely and consciously practical part of Plato's political theory... He insists on the need for a general amity of Greece, he emphasises the idea of a common public law which regulates, or should regulate, the relations of the Greek states; and if he does not preach a crusade against Persia; he lays stress on the fundamental distinction between the Greek and all other peoples and he draws from that distinction the moral that the Greeks must behave towards one another with a restraint which they need not show to the other world."

From all his writings it becomes clear that though Plato makes his state absolute within, he is far from thinking that it is absolute, or free from limitation, in its external life. Of course, he had no idea of universal brotherhood, or common human society within which the state is contained and by which its Nation is conditioned. This idea could be found only later on in stoic philosophy and then among the Christians. His sense of brotherhood was confined to the Greek world. But, as Barker writes, "He has a clear conception that the Greek-world, at any rate is a single society, with a civility or comity of its own, to which all its members are bound to conform within this society, peace should rule; or, if there is war, war should be waged according to a humane ruler. Within this society again, there should be general recognition of the right of personal liberty; and Greek should be the slave of Greek. Plato believes, in a word, that there is a public law of Greece, and that all Greek states are bound by this law." Thus, Plato's conception of universal brotherhood is a narrow one, limited to the brotherhood of Greece alone.

In his 'Greek Political Theory — Plato and His Predecessors' Barker has given some glimpses of foreign relations of Plato in a beautiful manner.

20

Estimate of Plato

Plato is considered as the "father to the idealists, romanticists, revolutionists and utopians of political philosophy" according to Maxey. In fact Plato was the first systematic political thinker in the West. He was, indeed, the father of political radicalism. As an idealist he aimed at creating an ideal State where justice and virtue should reign high under the fostering guidance and control of a Philosopher-King.

In order to achieve his objective he was even prepared to sacrifice the time honoured institution of private property and family life. But in his later years, he was forced by the conditions then prevailing, and his maturity of judgement, to modify his radicalism.

Though Plato has been often criticised for his hatred of democracy, the ideal of democracy is still far away from realisation fully even after more than two thousand years of his passing away.

Many of his ideas, such as communism of wives and communism of property were Utopian. If his communism of wives is impracticable in a modern nation-state, communism of property would be equally difficult to be fully realised in a modern state.

Many criticisms have been levelled against the ideas of Plato. While criticising many of his ideas, we must not forget that what Plato wrote was for his Greek City-State and not for a modern big state.

No wonder his emphasis on justice and functional specialisation, his feminism and his eugenics are features of ever-lasting interest in his political philosophy. Many of the conceptions of the middle ages are traceable to his Republic. Moore's 'Utopia' is more or less on the lines of Plato's Republic. The Renaissance and Humanist movements owe much to his ideas. In his conception of justice and communism he belongs to the school of utilitarians because he "puts the good of the community before everything else". This is given by R.L. Nettleship in a graphic manner — in his work on "Lectures on the Republic of Plato." Of course it is with Rousseau that Plato begins to exercise a steady influence on modern political philosophy. The German and English schools of Idealists owe much to him.

Besides his Republic we also find the modern notions of constitutionalism, of a mixed constitution and of the sovereignty of law traceable to the Laws of Plato.

As a matter of fact, Plato had a firm belief that he had found a way of life for people to live. Barker writes, "He never abandoned the belief that he had found a way of life; and he never ceased to train men to follow it, on the dream of that divine, if far-off, city, in whose institutions and system of education it should be permanently established as a common possession of men."

Prof. Jaszi, C.C. Maxey and McIlwain have appreciated and applauded the communism of property of Plato while comparing it with modern (economic) communism. Maxey feels that "virtually all socialistic and communistic thought has its roots in Plato." As such he further asserts that if Plato "were alive today he would be the reddest of reds" and no doubt he would go to Russia "with the same expectant enthusiasm as he displayed in answering the call of the ancient tyrant of Syracuse."

About Plato's importance, Maxey writes, "There was much in Plato of the ephemeral and the provincial, but the midrib of his political philosophy was timeless and universal. As a Greek of the post-Periclean period he was an anti-expansionist, a disbeliever in democracy, a condoner of slavery, a foe of commercialism, and an admirer of Lacedaemonian militarism; but as an analyst of social and political philosopher, reconstructive political theories and radical political programmes which have appeared in subsequent ages."

Something of Plato is to be seen in all the Utopias, and many of the authors of the imaginary commonwealth are hardly more than second rate imitators of the great Athenian dreamer and thinker. Maxey further writes, "Nearly all melioristic thought, especially that favouring education and eugenics as the most practicable modes of battering human society, reaches back to Plato. Milton, Locke, Rousseau, Goethe and other great apostles of social idealism have drawn heavily upon him. His mordant analysis of the fatal tendencies of free enterprise in an acquisitive society has been echoed again and again in the history of Western civilisation." Virtually all socialistic and communistic thought has its roots in Plato.

Plato's analysis of the factors in the growth and decline of States and their cycles of change reveals a genuine appreciation of the materialistic forces of historical causation. One would be surprised to know that there is a lot of Plato in the Soviet system of communism today.

According to Ebenstein, "In the whole history of Western philosophy no one has exercised as much influence as Plato. He is the founder of philosophical idealism, one of two or three major schools of philosophy dominating Western thought in the past as in the present."

According to Doyle, "Plato showed the necessity of considering the purpose of not only the state, but of man, before political life could hope to obtain any proper adjustments."

Finally, it is better and fitter we close this chapter by quoting Maxey who writes : "Simply to recognise that after a lapse of time which has rubbed out the achievements of unnumbered hosts of men who have won wars, built empires, amassed fabulous fortunes, invented amazing machines, written books of vast acclaim and done other deeds of high renown, the ideas of the prodigious principal of the first Academy still holds sway over the minds of men, is greater praise than any lavish out-pouring of adjectives could bestow."

Bibliography

A.R.M. Murray, *An Introduction to Political Philosophy.*

Bhandari and Sethi, *Plato and Aristotle.*

C.C. Maxey, *Political Philosophies.*

Durant Will, *The Story of Philosophy.*

E.Barker, *Greek Political Theory Plato and His Predecessors.*

E. Barker, *Political Thought of Plato and Aristotle.*

Edman Irwin, *The Philosophy of Plato.*

F.W. Coker, *Readings in Political Philosophy.*

G.H. Sabine, *A History of Political Theory.*

Natrop, *Plato's State and The Idea of Social Education.*

R.L. Nettleship, *Lectures on the Republic of Plato.*

B. Jowett, Translated by *Plato's Republic.*

K.R. Popper, *The Open Society.*

M.B. Foster, *Masters of Political Thought from Plato to Machiavelli.*

P. Doyle, *A History of Political Thought.*

R.H.S. Crossman, *Plato Today.*

W.A. Dunning, *A History of Political Theories — Ancient and Medieval.*

W. Ebenstein, *Political Thought in Perspective.*

W. Ebenstein, *An Introduction to Political Philosophy.*

C.L. Wayper, *Political Thought.*

A.E. Taylor, *Plato — The Man and his works.*

R.G. Gettell, *History of Political Thought.*

Constanstine, *Ritter, The Essence of Plato's Philosophy.*

G.C. Field, *The Philosophy of Plato.*

C.H. McIlwain, *The Growth of Political Thought in the West.*

A.E. Zimmern, *The Greek Commonwealth.*

Gomperz, *Greek Thinkers.*

G. Lowes Dickenson, *The Greek View of Life.*

W.W. Willoughby, *The Political Theories of the Ancient World.*

J.P. Mayer, *Political Thought : European Traditions.*

BIBLIOGRAPHY

B. Jowett, Edited by *The Dialogues of Plato.*

Philip Leon, *Plato.*

Grote, *Plato.*

A.E. Taylor, Translated by — *The Laws of Plato.*

R.W. Livingstone, Edited by — *The Legacy of Greece.*

G.L. Myers, *The Political Ideas of the Greeks.*

INDEX